Legal Almanac Series No. 67

HOW TO BE A WITNESS

By
Kevin Tierney

1971
OCEANA PUBLICATIONS, INC.
Dobbs Ferry, New York

Library of Congress Catalog Card Number: 79-170975

International Standard Book Number: 0-379-11080-6

Also by Kevin Tierney:
  Courtroom Testimony: A Policeman's Guide, published
  in 1970 by Funk & Wagnalls.

Manufactured in the United States of America

CONTENTS

CONTENTS (continued)

INTRODUCTION

Few of the thousands of people who are called as witnesses each year have any but a vague notion of the function which they are about to serve. All too frequently they are never enlightened because court officials, lawyers and others who might explain it to them are busy with more pressing matters. This is why many witnesses are filled with trepidation at the thought of testifying; they are victims of the fear of the unknown. Lawyers forget how awesome the machinery of justice looks to a layman and leave witnesses to find out for themselves what part they play in the overall legal process. This book is designed to help those many baffled people gain some insight into the legal system which has called them away from their everyday pursuits.

A witness sees the legal process at work from a strange perspective. As likely as not, he has no particular interest in the outcome of the litigation in which he appears; chance ordained that he would know something useful to one party or another. Furthermore, he will probably only see that part of the proceedings in which he himself gives evidence and the total pattern of a trial will not be apparent to him. There are witnesses who have left the witness-stand feeling that no pattern exists at all, so bewildering has been their experience.

In these pages, a reader will not find anything like a comprehensive explanation of trials and legal technique, but some of the major characteristics of a witness's experience are explained. It is hoped that a prospective witness will find what he reads here valuable when he gives evidence, and someone who has already given evidence will achieve added insight into what happened during his appearance as a witness. From the lawyer's point of view, these pages may hopefully prove useful as a summary handbook and afford some insights into a witness's mental processes and psychology.

Ideally, this book will be read as soon as a subpoena has been received--and it is with receipt of a subpoena that a witness's journey into the labyrinths of the law really begins.

KEVIN TIERNEY

Chapter I

THE SUBPOENA

The first formal intimation that a person may be called as a witness is receipt of a document known as a subpoena, and the fact that one has been issued is a sign that litigation has begun in earnest. A subpoena is a command to the person to whom it is directed to appear on a specified date at a given time and place for the purpose of testifying. In addition it may require the recipient to bring with him documents or other materials that are expected to be useful in the proceedings to which he is summoned.

The Power of Subpoena

The power to compel the attendance of potential witnesses is vested in courts of law (and related bodies such as grand juries which act under the authority of a court), Congress and most regulatory agencies, like the Interstate Commerce Commission, which have been given it by statute. It follows from this that receipt of a subpoena does not necessarily augur an appearance in court, but can be a summons from a large number of different sorts of body. There are great differences between appearing before a court and appearing before other bodies, the major one being that only courts abide by the rules of evidence. Even grand juries, with their close historic association with the courts, are not bound by evidentiary rules and may, for instance, present an indictment based upon hearsay.

Although the power to issue subpoenas is vested with the courts and certain other bodies, it is characteristically exercised at the request of a party to litigation who believes that his case will be aided by the people to whom he wants subpoenas to be addressed. It is basic to the conduct of both civil and criminal trials that the courts should lend their subpoena power to litigants and the practice has a long history. The Sixth Amendment to the Constitution provides that: "In all criminal prosecutions the accused shall

1

enjoy the right . . . to have compulsory process for obtaining witnesses in his favour . . . ."

The existence of the subpoena power ensures that even an unpopular litigant can force witnesses to come to court, rather than making their attendance a matter of mere whim or caprice. The duty to testify is a public one, and evidence may not be withheld because of emnity or the personal inconvenience involved in providing it. In practice many witnesses volunteer their aid to litigants and would appear willingly--but the best practice is to serve them with a subpoena nonetheless to discourage them from changing their minds.

The Nature and Content of a Subpoena

A subpoena is <u>not</u> an order to give evidence but only an order to attend <u>for the purpose</u> of giving evidence; whether that purpose will be fulfilled can never be foreseen: the case may be settled before it even gets to court, or counsel may decide at the last moment that his client's interest is not served by calling the person he has caused to be subpoenaed. The latter possibility is rarely encountered in practice, but where it is, a bad tactical error has generally been made by the lawyer concerned because it gives the opposition the chance to call the witness and bring out in open court the fact that the other side was "scared" of putting him on the stand. The inference that the court is invited to draw is, of course, that the witness would have said things unfavorable to the cause of the party who had compelled his attendance.

The obligation to testify does not arise until a witness has actually been sworn in court and it follows from this that service with a subpoena carries no assurance of having the opportunity to do so. Many recipients of subpoenas have attended court blithely (and incorrectly) assuming that their share of the limelight is assured, only to find that they have waited uncomfortably in the corridors of the courthouse for a call which never came.

A subpoena will give the name of the court or other body by which it is issued, the title of the proceedings for which the addressee is being summoned, the date upon which it was issued and the place, date and time at which he must present himself. In most states there is no requirement that a subpoena must be issued a certain minimum time in advance of the proceedings; a prospective

2

witness may be served a subpoena and immediately taken to court, a state of affairs that means a witness may be taken unawares, although in general he will have adequate notice.

A subpoena is valid if it is addressed to a person by the name he is known by, even though it is not his real or "legal" name. It is also permissible for a subpoena to be issued reciting a string of names linked by the abbreviation "a/k/a", meaning "also known as", if the witness wanted has been known by various names.

In some states, a subpoena must be accompanied by money or travel vouchers sufficient to pay its recipient's expenses in attending, but it is more usual today for the form of subpoena to include a notice promising reimbursement upon appearance. This matter can be important when a distant witness whose expenses are likely to be heavy is served. If no remittance is enclosed with the subpoena and no promise of payment is made, a recipient should get one or the other before the hearing.

Some jurisdictions call subpoenas "witness summonses" or "appearance orders" but this difference in name has no legal significance.

Service of a Subpoena

A litigant who wishes to secure the attendance of a witness at court must serve him with a subpoena if there is to be any legal obligation on him to attend; it will be of no avail to show that the witness had actual knowledge that he was wanted at court. The whole purpose of subpoenas is to provide an exclusive and recognized means of imposing a duty to attend and service of one is the only device appropriate. Service must be in the proper manner and that varies from state to state. A recipient of a subpoena to attend court should check the local rules carefully to see whether they have been complied with; in service of process there is many a slip between cup and lip.

The two common methods of service are personal service and service by mail.

PERSONAL SERVICE. Some jurisdictions insist that subpoenas be served by actual delivery into the hands of the addressee by an authorized process-server. An authorized process-server may be a full-time professional who does nothing but serve legal papers for his living or he may be a policeman, or court clerk, or other person designated by the court. Proof of service is achieved when the process-server executes an affidavit stating that he did indeed hand the document to the proper person. Sometimes, a citizen will find himself in trouble for failing to obey a subpoena or other court notice that he has never received, because of a disreputable practice known as "sewer service" by which a process-server swears a false affidavit of personal service. In 1971, a high official of a professional servers' association was convicted in New York City of making false affidavits of service so that he could collect fees for work he had never actually done. A person who finds himself the victim of such a fraud should not only protest to the relevant court, but should consult an attorney with a view to bringing an action for damages against the process-server concerned. The amount recoverable will be large indeed where the law awards "exemplary" or "punitive" damages for such cases.

In most states a person commits no offense by using his ingenuity to avoid service of a subpoena. He may simply run away from the process-server, or adopt a more elaborate strategy like disguising himself, or going into hiding, or leaving the jurisdiction. A process-server who is defeated in his aim by a wily prospective witness may apply to the court for a "witness warrant" to arrest him, but this is not a criminal warrant; it is part of the machinery of civil justice.

It should be noted that a witness who contemplates leaving the jurisdiction to avoid a subpoena is acting alone, for Disciplinary Rule 7-109(B) of the American Bar Association's Code of Professional Responsibility forbids a lawyer from advising a person to leave the jurisdiction of a tribunal for the purpose of making him unavailable as a witness.

There are some limits to the lengths to which one may to go avoid service, as the case of a lady from Houston, Texas, illustrates. When an attempt was made to serve a subpoena on her relating to a civil suit she bit the hand of the process-server, causing him considerable pain and suffering and for that she was jailed for thirty days and fined $280.

There are problems, too, for a person who intends to leave the jurisdiction to avoid service, at least if the courts get wind of the plan in advance. Many states (including New York) and the federal courts have authority to require prospective witnesses to give surety for their appearance which will be forfeited on non-

4

appearance. Rule 46(b) of the Federal Rules of Criminal Procedure for the United States District Courts (followed in many states) has the following provision, which is fairly typical for all jurisdictions:

"If it appears by affidavit that the testimony of a person is material in any criminal proceeding and if it is shown that it may become impracticable to secure his presence by subpoena, the court or commissioner may require him to give bail for his appearance as a witness, in an amount fixed by the court or commissioner. If the person fails to give bail the court or commissioner may commit him to the custody of the marshal pending final disposition of the proceeding in which the testimony is needed, may order his release if he has been detained for an unreasonable length of time and may modify at any time the requirement as to bail."

It will be seen that the wording of this rule (and others like it in other jurisdictions) gives the court considerable discretion. Not only can the power be used to bail a witness who is known to intend to leave the jurisdiction, but there is no requirement that such an intention be shown; all that need be shown is that it "may" become impracticable to secure a person's presence by subpoena. In practice, the power is sparingly exercised.

Most of the law relating to personal service grew up in an era which had no public mail service and therefore personal delivery of some kind or another had to be made if a witness was to hear of the proceedings at all. Even today, however, personal service has the great advantage that it ensures that the person concerned truly gets notice of his obligation to attend court in a way that no other form of service does. One of the regrettable aspects of non-personal service (discussed in the following section) is that the very ease with which a litigant can make it encourages some irresponsible blanket uses of subpoenas, so that many more people are inconvenienced by having to attend court than is strictly necessary.

It is perhaps appropriate to point out that a person who has been served a subpoena which he believes not to be justified by the value of the evidence (if any) he can give is always entitled to contact the party for whom he is called in advance of the pending proceedings and seek to obtain an agreement to dispense with his testimony. This avoids the inconvenience of attending court much more simply than ignoring the subpoena and running the risk of subsequent arrest.

In the absence of specific statutory authority, service cannot be achieved by leaving a subpoena at a person's "last known address", or with a relation or an employer. Where these forms of service are permitted, the fact that it was not actually received is a defense to the charge of non-appearance.

SERVICE BY MAIL. Nowadays, many states permit service by mail, thereby eliminating the costly necessity of personal service. Service by mail is known in several states as "substituted service", a name which indicates that it is a substitute for actual service. The use of "substituted service" has given rise to much legal dispute and is by no means as easy as it sounds. In the majority of cases, the addressee will turn up at court at the appointed time without raising technical objections, but a person who wishes to challenge the service will often find it fruitful to consider carefully whether the circumstances of the delivery are compatible with the rules.

The first point is that nearly all state statutes which permit service by mail specify the use of certified mail and therefore a subpoena received by first-class or air mail may, if desired, be ignored.

Secondly, the very statutes that require that certified mail be used often do not say whether the sender must have a post-office stamped certificate of posting. This is important because blank gummed slips for certified mail are available at any post office and can be filled in by anyone; but for proof that the item was actually posted it is necessary to take it to the post office and get the slip franked. Similarly, statutes often do not provide whether a service by mail is valid if no return receipt signed by the addressee has been obtained. If it is not specified as necessary a good argument can still be made that without it service is invalid. If it is required, the addressee can refuse to sign a receipt, in which case the subpoena will be returned to sender by the post office.

The third difficulty caused by service by mail arises from delivery on a Sunday or a public holiday. Mail is not often delivered on Sunday, but it is near Christmastide or if an item is sent special delivery, and most states prohibit service on Sunday. Many states also prohibit service on a public holiday, and since some state holidays are not recognized by the federal government, the Post Office continues to deliver mail on those days. Any subpoena received on such days is invalidly served in those states.

Subpoena of Out-of-State Witnesses

A state court has no power outside the boundaries of its jurisdiction and its subpoenas are impotent to compel witnesses living elsewhere. It is for this reason that, as mentioned earlier, a prospective witness seeking to avoid having to testify may leave a state whose courts have a subpoena out for him. In an effort to thwart such evasions nearly every state has passed the Uniform Act to Secure the Attendance of Witnesses from without a State in Criminal Proceedings, which sets up machinery by which any state which has passed the Act will cooperate in helping any other state with a similar Act on its books to get the witnesses it wants. A state wishing to secure a witness (referred to in the Uniform Act as "the requesting state") asks the state in which he is to be found ("the requested state") to issue an order requiring him to attend the proceedings in the requesting state. A judge in the requested state will issue an order if he is satisfied that:

1. it will not cause the person concerned undue hardship to appear in the requesting state;
2. that, if he does appear, he will be a material witness; and
3. the laws of the requesting state and any other through which he must pass will protect him from arrest and service of civil and criminal process.

These provisions deserve some comment. A judge in the requested state will not be prevented from issuing an order because it will cause the person concerned inconvenience or loss of earnings; hardship must be shown. The requesting state need not satisfy the judge in the requested state that the potential witness is an important one; only that he is material; the witness need not be shown to be indispensable. Finally, the judge must be satisfied that the laws of the requesting state and any state on the way protect the person concerned from arrest or service but there is no remedy available if the judge turns out to be wrong. If New York requests Michigan to order a witness to go to New York, the witness may have to pass through Ohio to do so. The judge may look at Ohio law and decide that Ohio does not permit arrest or service of a person travelling through in such circumstances; but he may be mistaken. In this connection, it may be noted that the Uniform Act does not contain a provision to the effect that subscribing states will prohibit arrest or service of a person travelling through their territories in response to an order issued under the Act. This omission could be very important to someone wanted as a witness who is also suspected of crime, or involved in civil litigation.

The Uniform Act operates only on the basis of reciprocity; that is, the requested state will normally only be bound by its provisions if the requesting state has adopted the Uniform Act itself. If the requesting state has not there may still be some alternative provision under the requested state's law under which an order can be made regardless of reciprocity, but such a provision (probably an old one) will have different procedures and less certainty of success than under the Uniform Act. Furthermore, there are a few states which habitually do not surrender witnesses to other states.

Failure to Obey a Subpoena

A failure to obey a subpoena may result in the issuance of a "witness warrant", ordering the arrest of the witness. In addition, if the failure to answer the subpoena cannot be excused, the arrestee may be punished for contempt of court. On the other hand, the court wants the subject's testimony and providing it gets that it is not normally disposed to punish. However, the power to punish by fine or imprisonment or both does exist.

A person who procures a witness warrant by untruly alleging that a subpoena had previously been properly served on a prospective witness will be open to an action for malicious or "false"

8

arrest if as a consequence the prospective witness is arrested pursuant to the witness warrant.

The only class of person who can legally ignore a subpoena is comprised of holders of diplomatic immunity. A diplomat cannot be touched by the legal process of the foreign state in which he serves unless he waives his immunity, a matter entirely within his discretion. Diplomats customarily claim their immunity in writing as soon as they receive notice of the proceedings for which they have been summoned.

Discharge of Obligation Imposed by Subpoena

A subpoena only imposes a duty to attend the relevant proceedings, not to testify. However, that obligation is not discharged by attending and immediately leaving; a subpoenaed witness must hold himself available until it has been indicated that he is no longer required and free to go.

Much confusion sometimes arises when proceedings are adjourned or "continued", because a subpoena summons a person for a particular date or time and does not contemplate the possibility of delay or that the court will re-convene at a later date to consider the same matter. When this happens specific instructions should be sought from a court official. The basic rule is that if the directions on the face of the subpoena have been complied with, nothing more is required.

Most witnesses have the happy experience of fulfilling their duty in a day, and then being free to return to normal life. However, it is sometimes true that a witness can be kept away from his home and work for weeks at a court far away from his locality. This can happen when he is called for a date representing the expected beginning of a trial although his evidence is not called for until it is well underway, or where he gives evidence quite promptly, but is instructed by the judge to remain available until he is discharged. A witness should not leave a court after giving evidence without making sure that he will not be called on again, either because a party may obtain permission to recall him to rectify an oversight or for the purposes of rebuttal. It is safest to ask the judge whether one is free to go. If it turns out that there is an obligation to remain, a witness is entitled to all his living expenses while away from home while giving testimony, at actual cost, providing the standard of living is one approved by the court.

Chapter II

FINANCIAL RIGHTS OF WITNESSES

The pecuniary rewards of being an ordinary witness are negligible. In most states provision is made for reimbursement of any out-of-pocket expenses in attending court, though these are often calculated on a basis less than actual cost, so the witness may even lose on those! As suggested in Chapter I, dealing with subpoenas, a witness should not embark on a long journey to give evidence unless the subpoena contains sufficient funds to get him to court and back, or he secures an official undertaking to reimburse him.

In some states, a witness is entitled to an additional payment, calculated on a daily, or half-day scale, for the time he spends attending court. This does not relate to the time he is on the witness-stand, but to the time he is compelled to wait at court for his turn to come. The payment provides some consolation for the waste of his time and loss of earnings from his regular work. However, payment for this purpose is always woefully inadequate and insufficient to compensate anyone who earns at modern rates; the court scales were drawn many years ago and have not been updated. The unfairness of this inadequacy is mitigated for many people called as witnesses by their employers' willingness to pay them their normal wages or salary while they are acting as witnesses, so that they lose nothing financially, but witness duty weighs very heavily upon self-employed people who lose their earning power while away from their business. It is also a burden to women with young children who must find someone else to look after them while they are away at court. Salesmen whose major compensation comes from commission are also put at a disadvantage when they are called as witnesses.

The deplorable state of affairs has been strongly criticized by the President's Commission on Law Enforcement and Administration of Justice which reported:

> "In one urban court witnesses receive 75 cents
> a day . . . . This economic sacrifice by wage
> earners and small businessmen cannot be justi-
> fied as a duty of citizenship or on any other
> ground."

In view of this, the Commission recommended increases in the
witness payments made, but did not specify the scale of these
increases that it thought desirable. Unfortunately, as the Commission itself recognized: "Almost all of the specific recommendations made . . . will involve increased budgets [for the federal
government] . . . . The States, the cities, and the counties also
will have to make substantial increases in their contributions to
the system . . . ." Since nearly every agency of government at
every level in the United States is currently in a fiscal crisis
that shows no signs of solution, there is little hope that the Commission's recommendations will be generally implemented.

The dilemma is compounded by the ethical and other restrictions placed on payment of witnesses by the parties. Even if a
party is willing to supplement the public recompense offered to
an ordinary witness, the path is fraught with danger. The difficulties are well brought out by Ethical Consideration 7-28 pro-
mulgated by the American Bar Association as part of its Code of
Professional Responsibility, which reads in part:

> "Witnesses should always testify truthfully and
> should be free from any financial inducements that
> might tempt them to do otherwise. A lawyer
> should not pay or agree to pay a non-expert wit-
> ness an amount in excess of reimbursement for
> expenses and financial loss incident to his being
> a witness . . . . (I)n no event should a lawyer
> pay or agree to pay a contingent fee to any wit-
> ness.

The problem that the A.B.A. is here wrestling with is that an offer to a witness to pay him an amount which might be looked upon
as a profit might also be looked upon as approaching a bribe. A
payment made to a witness which was "contingent" on the success
of the party making the payment in a litigation obviously is an

11

encouragement to the witness to trim his testimony in that party's favor.

It ought also to be said that if a witness is subpoenaed to testify by one side and finds himself offered money, or gifts or other benefits by the other side, he should immediately report the matter to the court; this, too, is highly unethical and is a practice which has been expressly disapproved in Re Robinson, 151 App. Div. 589, 136 N.Y.S. 458 (1912), affirmed 209 N.Y. 354, 103 N.E. 160 (1913).

All the comments above about the financial rights of a witness are applicable only to a witness who has been served with a subpoena. A witness who attends court of his own free will is not entitled to the various statutory payments for expenses or compensation for loss of earnings and living expenses. It is therefore in the interests of a prospective witness to be subpoenaed, even though he would have attended voluntarily, so that the statutory right to payment accrues to him.

As was mentioned in Chapter I, it can happen that, for a variety of reasons, a person subpoenaed as a witness is never called, with the unhappy result that he has spent hours and even days waiting for a summons that never came. In these circumstances, he is nevertheless entitled to recompense. A witness is paid to attend court, not to give evidence, and the fact that he was never brought to the witness-stand is quite irrelevant to his rights; providing he has attended at the command of the court, he will be treated just as if he had given evidence.

Up to now, this discussion of the financial rights of witnesses has dealt only with "ordinary" witnesses. But there is a privileged category of witness who is nearly always paid: the expert witness. The expert witness is one who is brought to the stand to do something that most ordinary witnesses are forbidden to do: give his opinion on some issue, rather than merely give the facts as he observed them. The commonest sort of expert witness is probably a doctor, though from time to time experts in fingerprints, ballistics, handwriting and other matters are to be found. These experts do not merely describe facts, but they draw inferences from them and reach conclusions. These conclusions are valuable to the court, but they are only opinions. Even expert opinions can disagree and it is common for a party to litigation to scout around to find an expert who is of an opinion convenient to his view of a case. He usually finds one. These witnesses are almost always paid handsomely for their services and some of them make a profession of giving expert evidence in court. Cross-examination usually reveals the fact of payment and the sum involved, which can be quite large. An ordinary witness who had received payment from the party on whose side he was appearing would be subject to impeachment for interest in the same way as an expert witness; the other side would argue that the receipt of money indicated that the witness might be stretching his testimony to favor the side that paid him. It is true that some experts have been regarded as extremely flexible in their testimony, to the extent that they have been suspended of acting simply as paid mouthpieces for hire, although most experts are no doubt ethical and reliable. It will be noted that expert witnesses are recognized as exceptions to Ethical Consideration 7-28 of the Code of Professional Responsibility referred to above.

Chapter III

THE CAPACITY TO OBSERVE

The law depends on human observation for nearly all of its factual data and for this reason witnesses have been described as "the eyes and ears of justice". But it is a great mistake to place too much faith in the accuracy of human observation; many of the clearest miscarriages of justice have been caused by erroneous, though honest, observations. These can arise from all sorts of causes--the perspective from which a witness saw the things he described, the conditions in which he saw them, and so on--but the fundamental difficulty arises because human beings are not as well equipped for observation as they might be and they are not as good at it as they believe.

A witness giving evidence in court is actually involved in a quite complex mental activity, in which there are many opportunities for error. Put succinctly, it may be said that a witness is describing his memory of an event which he observed at some time in the past. From this, we can see that error may arise from three major causes: (1) a witness's initial observation of the event in question may have been faulty; (2) his memory may be inaccurate; (3) his description of his memory may be inadequate and misleading. In view of the importance of testimony, each of these possible sources of error will now be considered in turn. One of the greatest human delusions is an absolute faith in memory and it is the one which can do the most harm if a witness does not appreciate how fallible memory is.

Modern biologists agree that human beings are rather poorly endowed with sense organs by the standards of the animal kingdom. It is through the sense organs that we observe the outside world and this fact should at once alert us to the danger that humans do not receive full data about "what happens" because their apparatus is crude. Everyone knows that a really powerful radio, equipped with wavebands which permit fine tuning, can receive many signals that will not be picked up by a small transistor. The owner of a transistor would be gravely mistaken if he believed that the only transmissions were those which his small receiver could monitor. By analogy to the human sense organs, we may say that a human being would be gravely mistaken if he thought that the only things that were going on around him were those that he could monitor. A little thought will show that any such conclusion is false. We cannot see the planets like Pluto which are at the furthest edges of the solar system, but they exist. We cannot see the millions of germs in the atmosphere, but they too exist. The list of matters which human beings cannot observe unaided could be a very long one. We shall later draw some important conclusions from this limitation on human powers, but first simple biology will aid us in understanding the dimensions of the problem.

Humans are able to receive "signals" from the outside world in five ways: through the eyes, ears, nose, skin and mouth. Through at least three of these possibilities, it is demonstrable that human equipment is inferior to that of other members of the animal kingdom, and it is probable that the other two also display less sensitivity in humans than other animals.

First, the eyes of a human being are demonstrably inferior to those of birds like the falcon and the hawk, which can see their prey from a great height. Humans also lack special abilities of sight, like seeing in the dark which felines and owls possess. Similarly, dogs have superior senses of hearing and smell to humans. There are whistles that make a noise heard by dogs which are totally outside the hearing of human beings. Yet, once again to emphasize the relevance of these things to testimony, it would be a false conclusion for a human being to draw that when the whistles were blown there was silence. Tracker dogs can follow living creatures by the scent they leave, although people have poor senses of smell and in some cases, none at all. It is a measure of how little humanity relies upon its sense of smell that a person without it is scarcely regarded as afflicted at all, whereas a person who is blind or deaf receives sympathy and special treatment. The reason for this is that a sense of smell is not necessary to survival in modern conditions of civilization, while someone who lacks sight or hearing is at a severe disadvantage. It can be said that the ability to smell is (biologically) a redundant one in humans nowadays.

15

The fourth and fifth senses--taste and touch--are both well developed in humanity and are those most difficult to compare with other living things. There is evidence that some animals have greater sensitivity in these areas than mankind, but since these senses are relatively rarely in question in courts of law, there is no need to discuss it here; the point has been made that our species is by no means the best endowed with sense organs.

This having been recognized, the reader may well ask how it comes to pass that humanity has attained its indisputable dominance over the earth. The answer is simple, but it is not to be found in human sense equipment: the human brain is vastly superior to that of its nearest animal rivals and more than compensates for the inferiority of eyes, ears and nose. The brain permits humans to use intelligence to deduce what has happened even if they did not receive signals which told them directly. This is a major part of what is called "intelligence", and indeed that quality can be defined as the ability to arrive at a true conclusion without having actually observed the truth. When the sense organs have missed something, or been unable to transmit it in sufficient detail, the brain supplies logical "fillers" to the gaps left by poor observation. This function of the brain can be demonstrated by many scientifically-devised tests, some of which have particular relevance to the use of witnesses in the courtroom. But a practical demonstration of this phenomenon can be gleaned from watching a conjurer who amuses us by doing "impossible" things, like producing eggs from nowhere, or "reading" our minds after we have selected a playing card. Nearly all the standard magic tricks depend upon illusion created in the minds of the audience deliberately by the magician. He is not tricked, but we are just because our brains fill the logical gaps left by our observation.

It is an interesting sidelight upon psychology that the brain is most baffled when logic points in two unpalatable directions, and once again this can be illustrated by a look at the magician's art. One of the most famous tricks ever presented has been sawing a lady in half. Here, the audience sees the magician saw through a woman's body, encased in a box from which her head protrudes at one end and her feet at the other. Nevertheless, after the sawing is completed, she steps from the box unharmed. The audience, having seen this performance, has really only two alternatives to believe: (1) that somehow the lady has an immunity to the normal rule that humans do not emerge unscathed from being cut through the middle, or (2) that in spite of appearances, she was not really sawn in half at all. The applause that a conjurer earns is for his ability to fool his audience; there is no fun in the spectacle if it is clear how the trick is done.

Although we are prepared to applaud the deceptive magician, we do not usually learn the lesson that our observation is not to be wholly relied upon and in everyday life remain "sure" of the most unsure things. Intellectually, we find it difficult to accept the fallibility of our own observation, because it is a natural trait to deny that one is wrong. It is for this reason that no man should be allowed to be judge of his own credibility, and self-serving declarations of honesty and accuracy deserve little weight. Yet we should constantly be on our guard against the easy assumption that what happened was what we think happened. There are a number of special situations in which there is a likelihood of error, among them being events that are quick and without prior warning; confused or unusual; without any discernable rhyme or reason; disgusting, horrifying or the kind from which it is natural to recoil; or those which are one of a number of similar occurrences within a short time. Of course, this list is by no means exhaustive and nearly every event has the potential for faulty observation. But these circumstances are the kind where it has been found through scientific experiment the brain unconsciously jumps to conclusions which, though they may be right, can easily be wrong. A striking practical illustration of the possibility of error in situations containing the elements listed above comes from the report of the Warren Commission on the death of President John F. Kennedy. The Commission reported:

> "The consensus among the witnesses at the scene was that three shots were fired. However, some heard only two shots, while others testified that they heard four and prehaps as many as five or six shots."

We may take it for granted that all the witnesses had the ability to count; the problem was that they were unable to register the sudden, fast-moving horror of what was happening. Incidentally, it is worth noting that the Commission draws a quite false inference from the facts before it; it speaks of a "consensus among the witnesses", but no consensus existed, because the witnesses disagreed. A consensus is "a collective unanimous opinion of a number of persons; a general agreement, "(dictionary definition). To describe an important disagreement on the number of shots fired as a "consensus" that three were fired is a grievous fallacy. Nevertheless, the statement does highlight how it is that fundamental disagreements about facts can arise.

The trouble with this realization is that it casts doubt on the value of nearly all courtroom testimony. After all, many cases turn upon facts of just such a kind that will be inadequately observed. This is particularly true of many serious criminal trials, where the facts are in one way or another unpalatable and sensational. What hope is there for justice, if its eyes and ears are so little to be relied upon? The answer can only be in relative terms; human observation is given credence not because it is good, but because it is the best available. There is no other way of reconstructing the past for litigation purposes. Even those tangible relics that seemingly "tell the story" are of little use without testimony. That photograph of a husband and wife joyously holding hands together, for instance, might be taken to indicate a happy marriage, but it might be a misleading piece of pretense that all was well. Certainly, we cannot tell without confirmation from other sources that it was a happy marriage, for it is possible that immediately after the photograph was taken a bitter quarrel broke out. Similarly reservations are appropriate about documents; their significance depends greatly upon the circumstances in which they were made, and these can only be ascertained from testimony.

The reservations expressed about the value of testimony so far apply generally, and it is a pity that many jurymen and witnesses alike are unaware of them. In addition, there are special factors which can affect the accuracy of perception, the two most important of which are defects in the observer himself and adverse conditions for observation. Although there is much more awareness of the effects of these two possibilities than there is of the inherent limitations in our sensory equipment, insufficient attention is often paid to them in assessing a witness.

It is a rule of law that a party to litigation takes his witness as he finds him. If the witness happens to be a notorious liar,

18

the party must use his testimony with that in mind; the law will not make allowances for the trick of fate that gave the party an ill-reputed witness. In the same way, a litigant has to accept the consequences which follow from calling a witness who has poor vision, or hearing, or some other defect of relevance to his reliability. Occasionally, scientific evidence is on hand to show the court that a witness has defective eyesight, but this is rare and is never required as a basis for introducing a witness. Unless one side or another raises the issue, a witness will be assumed to have satisfactory vision. In truth, this is an unfounded assumption, for eye doctors know that the capacity to see varies widely among even healthy people of the same age and condition, and that large numbers of people walk around with defects in their sight of which they are not aware, or do not care about. A young murder suspect some years ago in New York was found to have only 20/200 vision which nears blindness, but he did not wear glasses. Then again, there are many people who suffer from color blindness without knowing it. Deafness, and particularly partial deafness, can lead to all sorts of misunderstandings and misapprehensions, and its victims can remain unaware of their affliction for years.

These deficiencies have the effect of increasing their sufferer's chances of making perceptual mistakes over and above the average. Any person who expects to be called as a witness who suffers from eye or hearing problems should tell the lawyers in the case in advance of the trial, for it may make a difference to them in planning their strategy. On the stand, such a witness should not hesitate to admit his afflictions--there is nothing discreditable in them--and neither should he be ashamed to admit that, as a result of them, he was not able to see or hear some part of an event. It is much better to do that than profess certainty about matters which have been only partially perceived. In a famous libel trial, a witness admitted he was a little deaf, and was cross-examined:

Q: Many things may have been said which you did not hear?

A: There was nothing vital that I would not have heard.

Q: If you did not hear it, how do you know whether it was vital or not?

The witness really could not give a satisfactory reply. This witness was no doubt an honest man; he was led to take a foolish position because he was unwilling to face the consequences of his deafness. How much better he would have fared if he had frankly admitted the limitation that nature had placed upon him. The delusion of certainty was mentioned earlier in this chapter as one of which witnesses should beware. Those with special impediments should be specially wary.

Apart from conditions of physical infirmity which are more or less permanent, special and self-induced temporary states have considerable bearing upon a witness's reliability, and will certainly be a relevant subject for cross-examination. A witness who, at the time of his observation, was under the influence of drink or drugs, or suffering from fatigue or extreme emotion, may have colored an event by adding to it in his mind's eye. Certainly, there is abundant evidence that alcohol alters the judgment of drivers of distance and speed and these may reasonably be classified for our purposes as perceptual changes.

The final major influence on powers of human observation is the conditions in which the observation is made. It does not need any great insight into science to know that an observation made in the dark will not be so reliable as one made in the noonday sun, particularly when it relates to detail and color. Common sense tells us that it is difficult to hear a conversation across a crowded room where lots of other people are talking at the same time. Adverse conditions case serious doubts upon observations made by even the most qualified witness and will be made much of by counsel on cross-examination; there is a lot of difference between watching a ball game from a front-row seat and seeing it from the stands.

Abnormal weather conditions like fog have a special relevance here and it is common practice for an attorney to hire a weather investigator in cases where weather conditions may be important. These investigators seek out people who were in the immediate vicinity when the litigated incident occurred and try to find witnesses who can contradict the opposition's version of the weather at the relevant time and place. Naturally, automobile accidents are most likely to give rise to this sort of investigation.

Altogether, the scientific evidence is that human beings are not good at observation; they are not well equipped for it, and are often unaware of their limitations. It is no wonder that, together with the problems of accurate memory and describing memory in words, testimony is fallible indeed. It is to these important topics that the next chapter is devoted.

Chapter IV

MEMORY AND RECALL

Since a witness is called before a court to recount the facts
in his possession, his powers of expression are heavily relied
on when he testifies; his knowledge is of no use unless it can be
communicated. A witness may be articulate, or he may be tongue-
tied; he may be quick-witted or slow; capable of bringing to life
what is in his memory or not--but what he says is all the court
has to go on. It is not enough that a witness exercises his capacity to observe; to be a good witness he must be able to memorize and recall accurately, under the formal conditons of a court
of law.

This is demanding a great deal from a witness. Even in perfect conditions for reminiscence, there are few people who can
produce a memory concisely and impartially. On the witness
stand, a witness may find himself facing a barrage of specific
questions, the answers to which he finds it almost impossible to
summon up. One of the defects of the question-and-answer method
by which testimony is elicited from witnesses is that the questions condition the answers so that much of what is relevant from
a witness's point of view is left out. Since most people remember
episodes or complete stories rather than isolated facts, many
witnesses leave the stand dissatisfied with their attempt to tell
what is in their minds.

Once an event has been observed it becomes added to the observer's experience through storage in the brain. This process
of storage is called memorizing and is most important for a witness. Unless experience was carried in the brain somehow, no
one could give an account of what happened in the past.

There is much scientific dispute about the workings of the
brain in memorizing experience. There is a school of thought that
believes that everything is memorized, so that every experience
stays with us deep in our unconscious, although it cannot be recalled totally because the brain engages in "suppressions" of

unpleasant memories. On the other hand, there are some who think that the capacity of the mind to take in memory is strictly circumscribed and in consequence useless information should not be committed to memory. This was the view of Sir Arthur Conan Doyle's famous character, Sherlock Holmes:

> "I consider that a man's brain originally is like an empty attic, and you have to stock it with such furniture as you choose . . . . It is a mistake to think that that little room has elastic walls and can distend to any extent. Depend upon it, there comes a time when for every addition of knowledge you forget something that you knew before."

Whatever the merits of the rival views of memory, it is clear that the process of combining memory and recall does not work evenly--that is to say, some facts are more easily recalled than others. This can be expressed by saying that memory itself is selective, or by saying that although memory is not selective, the ability to summon up material from the memory is variable. The truth must be left to scientists to decide, but the practical effect is the concern of any prospective witness: not everything is equally susceptible to recollection.

The first aspect of this phenomenon to be considered is that the brain acts as a censor of some unpleasant experiences. It occasionally happens that a patient undergoing a surgical operation is insufficiently anesthetized and wakes up while he is being operated on. In spite of this, he will not remember anything at all afterwards; the reason being that a brain has blacked out his memory of this traumatic experience. In the courtroom, the capacity of the brain to censor memory can sometimes be vividly demonstrated by the testimony of an accident victim who does not remember how the accident happened.

The way in which the brain "edits" memory is well-known to psychologists and refutes the view that memory is a neutral record of what happens. A famous novel was written in the 1930's which was made into a movie called "I Am a Camera". The author had deliberately tried to remain unmoved by the brewing Nazi revolution he saw, simply using his mind as an archive of observations uninfluenced by his personal feelings. Yet, finally, the most powerful impression left with the audience is his strong distaste for much of what he saw; his attempt at objectivity fails in the face of provocative subject matter. Hence, the illusion that because a person was present at some occurrence or other, he knows best what happened, and his recollections are to be relied upon, and that he can possibly recount the whole truth, is revealed. His internal censor and editor will have been working, even without his knowledge.

Aside from questions of brain censorship, there are involuntary eliminations of information stored in the brain according to what seems relevant. Only the salient features of a scene will be memorized; seemingly trivial detail will be lost forever. The trouble with this is that trivial details have a habit of gaining significance at a later date. A judgment of insignificance made by the brain at the time of an observation may be ill-considered, or data may come to light which puts the scene in a new perspective. What has been discarded as non-essential may turn out to be crucial at a later stage, as can be shown from everyday experience. There are many people who cannot remember the numbers of their automobile registration, or savings bank accounts, or other useful material. They must have seen those numbers many times; but the memory did not register them, knowing that they were always easy to check should the need arise. Yet if the automobile or savings account book is lost or stolen, those numbers it seemed unimportant to memorize suddenly become much desired information, and though they can probably be checked in other ways, it is convenient if they are simply remembered.

Ignorance is frequently rationalized by the excuse "I didn't have a chance to see," or some such remark--but, in truth, that is not the explanation. Rather, although the chance existed, and was taken, the data was not stored, leaving the memory with a void, or gap, which seems the same as never having had the opportunity to obtain the information in question. Educators are fully aware that their pupils have radically different rates of absorbtion in the classroom and that applies to people in general in all circumstances. At one extreme is found the possessor of a "photographic memory" (though we know from our consideration of "I Am a Camera" that this is strictly a misnomer) and at the other the scatter-brain type who never remembers anything. No one knows why the ability to memorize differs so much in different people, but there is no doubt that it does. It apparently has only a little to do with comprehension and intelligence, since there have been people able to learn by rote a great deal of material which they did not understand. Once more, it is worth noting that a litigant takes a witness as he is, not as he would wish the witness to be ideally, and there is little to be done about a bad memory.

Once information has entered the brain through one of the five sense organs it is not put in "cold storage". On the contrary, the brain apparently works on information it has memorized so that in many subtle ways, it is modified and changed. It is said, in recognition of this, that between lovers "absence makes the heart grow fonder." The reason for this is that the mind enhances the memory of the loved one during periods of enforced separation; the bad qualities are suppressed and the good ones exaggerated. Unhappiness is forgotten although joy is not. The result of this is that our "memories" are not true-to-life at all, but idealized versions of what really took place, usually idealized in a way that puts us in a good light and certainly does not feature ourselves as villains. In human memory, fact and fantasy become indistinguishably mingled so that much of what is "recalled" contains a strong spicing of wish-fulfillment. Although what a court of law wants to hear from a witness is the truth, the human mind does not readily hold the truth uncontaminated in storage, but adds and subtracts so that what is left bears a resemblance to the truth, but is not identical with it.

A particular example of the tricks memory can play is known as "superimposition". This occurs when the memory of two separate but comparable episodes is merged into one. Once this has happened it is impossible to disentangle one from the other and, if testified to, a superimposition casts doubt upon the accuracy of a witness's memory altogether. The motives underlying superimposition are not fully understood, but it may be a method of conserving brain effort in storing related material, or perhaps a way the total recollection can be made more vivid, though at the expense of exactness. Unfortunately, exactness is what is generally desired in the courtroom and an offer of vivid inaccuracy, even though the total impression may be fair, will meet a cold welcome. A kind of superimposition met with in court involves routine actions which the mind assumes to have been done. Suppose Peter has a safe in his office and makes a habit of checking it at the end of the day, just before he leaves, to make sure it is locked. One day there is a robbery. Peter may be convinced that he had checked the safe on the afternoon before, because he "always" did. But is that evidence enough? If he has no specific recollection that he did so (and the chances are that he will not) his certainty may be misplaced; he may have superimposed his practice of many previous days on the particular day of the crime.

This maverick attack on the accuracy of memory may disturb and even offend some prospective witnesses. Surely, they may ask, this cannot be a description of how _my_ mind works? This whole discussion seems to lead to the conclusion that all of us are to some extent deluded. It must be admitted that that is not an easy proposition to swallow--but it seems to be correct. What distinguishes "normal" and "abnormal" people is not that normal people are without fantasy and delusion, but that their delusions are confined to the past, not the present. There is nothing unusual in having false notions about one's personal history, but it is not normal to seriously misconceive the present. The memory can suffuse experience with a glow that comforts us without ill effects on our day-to-day functioning and is for most practical purposes harmless. In contrast, anyone who cannot separate fact and fantasy in the present has serious problems.

Not only is memory susceptible to distortion, but it is a variable ability, waxing and waning like the moon. The ability to recall a fact from storage is not one to be summoned up by an act of will, as can be deduced from the feeling that a wanted piece of information is "on the tip of one's tongue," but somehow cannot be brought out. Then again, it is common that a person remembers that there is something he must do, or refrain from doing, but cannot remember what it is; this is one aspect of absent-mindedness. People who so suffer resort to all sorts of reminders, like tying a knot in their handkerchief, but inherent in this procedure are two dangers: first, that they will omit to look at their handkerchief until too late, and second that even if they do so they will not remember why the knot was put there.

More general problems can arise with memories which have been disturbed by some external influence. The victims of brain damage, trauma and war-related injury such as "shell shock" can suffer total loss of memory, known as amnesia, or an extraordinarily enhanced ability to recall, often against their will. Horrific scenes keep springing to their minds, in a kind of "replay" which might normally be suppressed. It is also true that some accused criminals claim to know nothing about their actions at the relevant time, because "everything went black." Such a claim would not be dismissed out of hand as an excuse, for it is quite consistent with modern views of how the mind works under stress.

The fact that memory is inconstant is one that has great importance in a legal context, for it is shown time and again by inconsistent statements made by the same witness at different times. Witnesses often give statements soon after an incident has taken place, then later to lawyers who have been drawn into the matter by the prospect of litigation, and then they tell their story on the witness stand. Altogether, it is surprising if a witness can stick to precisely the same version of the incident on all three occasions. For the most part what he says will be the same, but there will generally be minor discrepancies between his recollection on one occasion and the next. Counsel for the client against whose interest the witness is testifying will probably brand the testimony as completely unreliable on the basis of these discrepancies, even though the bulk of the three accounts tallies. Only rarely does a witness to a crucial piece of evidence have his version accepted by both sides to a proceeding. Inconsistency in prior statements is what every lawyer prays for in the witnesses adduced by the other side, though he prays that his own will not suffer the same infirmity.

One more variable factor influences the evidence that a witness may provide; that is his ability to articulate what it is his memory has stored. Communication in words is at best a difficult process and some people find it exceptionally hard. We recognize the difficulty in some situations--for example, we all agree that "a picture is worth a thousand words." That adage is carried over to the courtroom when diagrams, maps and charts are shown to a jury instead of laboriously supplying background material through word descriptions. It happens that many of the issues that are litigated would become much simpler if only a picture were available, but since it is not, an eye-witness is the only alternative. His powers of description may be poor, his vocabulary woefully inadequate, and perhaps he stutters and splutters, too, but his memory is most valuable if it can be communicated.

27

The reconstruction of an experience in words nearly always involves some falsification. There is inevitably a rearrangement of the time sequence of an event during which two or more things were happening simultaneously. There is also an alteration of pace in describing something that happened quicker than it can be explained. There is nothing that can be done to avoid these sorts of distortions unless a new type of language is developed which communicates as rapidly as things really happen.

In addition to these problems, we find that words have shades of meaning which sometimes do not put across exactly what we mean to express, although there does not seem a better way of putting them. A dry description of an emotion-packed event may be quite misleading, but though we struggle for the appropriate words to recapture the atmosphere, they are elusive and we content ourselves with a pedestrian account which does not do justice to the truth. In this failing, no witness should reproach himself, for it is one which has troubled professional word-spinners and they have found no solution. The art of using language to recreate the past is given to few people in any large measure. It has been suggested that words impose a straitjacket because they require all experiences to be fitted into a relatively small number of available words; in everyday language only about 2,000 words are regularly used and it is true that some of them have an inbuilt imprecision about them. Different people mean different things when they use words like "fast", "big", "tall", "long" and "wide" and must be questioned carefully before their true meaning is revealed. These qualitative words are not as dangerous as they might be because there are universally accepted measures that can be applied to quantify them, such as miles per hour, or yards, feet or inches. But there are some words that express important ideas that cannot be qualified. Examples are descriptions like "the flower was red" or "his face was cruel." Redness and cruelty are variable qualities, not measurable upon any scale and when they are referred to on the witness stand they must be treated as the subjective descriptions they are.

A further difficulty of communicating what the brain has stored is that sometimes the association of ideas with particular words is different in the witness from the association made by his listeners. Most descriptive concepts can be communicated by several different and alternative words and sentences. The choice of words in ordinary speech is so quick that it is largely unconscious; words spring to our lips before we have consciously discarded alternatives. We may describe something as "red" though careful reflection might lead us to prefer "crimson" or "pink" as being more accurate. It needs little imagination to see that there are many other concepts which we express with a similar looseness in speech. Since the legal system of this country generally insists on evidence in oral rather than written form, spontaneous choices of description receive most emphasis.

Altogether, the arguments of the last two chapters have been enough to breed a healthy skepticism of witnesses. There is no entirely satisfactory means of reconstructing the past, even the very recent past, and no one connected with litigation should have too much faith in the ability of witnesses to give wholly correct accounts of what they saw, heard or otherwise experienced. After all, if people were wholly satisfactory recording machines, there would never be any conflict of evidence between people present at the same event. Our example relating to the number of shots fired at President Kennedy's assassination in the last chapter proves that it is not so. Differences of perspective and other factors can lead to utterly conflicting reports. Certainty is the greatest illusion of all.

Chapter V

COURTS AND THE SEARCH FOR TRUTH

It is quite wrong to think that courts spend most of their time deciding issues of law, for the majority of courts spend the majority of the time on questions of fact. Facts are deduced from the evidence that the courts hear, a major portion of which is provided by witnesses. Once the facts have been found the applicable rules of law are usually clear.

It seems axiomatic that courts should be concerned with the facts and to arrive at "the truth", whatever that may be, yet there are occasions when the law prefers falsehood to truth. Furthermore, as will be shown in this chapter, the procedures of American courts are in some ways ill designed to ensure that legal decisions are reached on a comprehensive view of the facts. Courts do not search for truth in any ordinary sense; the legal mind has an artificial construction of the truth which is molded by the technicalities of the law of evidence and which can, on occasion, cause the courts to follow a policy of wilful blindness.

Examples of the Preference for Falsehood

Many laymen find it difficult to believe that courts prefer to believe a lie than accept the truth and it is important to his understanding of the system he is entering that a prospective witness should have a grasp of this matter. The major examples in the Anglo-American jurisprudence are called "legal fictions" or "irrebuttable presumptions". An example will clarify matters. In all states there is an irrebuttable presumption that a child below a certain age (generally seven) lacks the capacity to commit a crime. It will make no difference if the prosecution finds ten witnesses to swear that a six-year-old was seen killing his mother with an ax; he cannot be convicted of murder or any other offense. Here, the law will deliberately ignore the facts. This example should be enough to warn a prospective witness that the courts are not always concerned with the truth, although it seeks from a witness a solemn oath "to tell the truth"!

Examples of Ignoring Truth

In just the same way as the court will occasionally act on a false premise quite deliberately, it will sometimes deliberately turn away from hearing the truth, even if by the ordinary rules of evidence the proferred matter is admissible. This can happen much more frequently than a court will adopt a legal fiction. There is a general discretion in a court to refuse to admit evidence which is competent and probative if its prejudicial effect is likely to be greater than its value as proof. This principle is routinely brought into play in criminal trials before a jury. Indeed, the historic reason for the development of rules of evidence was to prevent juries from hearing certain kinds of data, true though it might be. The most famous example is the prohibition on the prosecution telling a jury in a criminal trial that the accused has a record of previous convictions.

Procedural Barriers to Reaching the Truth

The responsibility of adducing evidence in the courts of the United States rests with the parties to litigation and although there is a residual power in the courts to make their independent inquiries it is obsolete and never exercised. Now, it is true that the parties should bear the burden of doing the spade work for litigation rather than the courts, but it is also true that the parties are highly interested in giving the facts a "slant". As a result, what the court hears is what one or the other of the parties wants it to hear that the other side cannot keep out. In doing battle under the adversary system of justice favored in this country, much relevant material may be swept under the carpet because neither side wants it revealed. This has a direct bearing on whether a witness is called, for if a witness is in possession of facts that both help and hinder one side's case, that side's lawyer wonders if he should call the witness at all. He may prefer not to call him, lose the favorable testimony but avoid the unfavorable. In this situation he can have several alternatives which he must balance in his mind to decide where his client's best interest is served:

1. he may call the witness on his client's behalf, elicit the favorable testimony in the witness's possession on direct examination and hope that his adversary will not succeed in

drawing out the damaging parts of the witness's testimony on cross-examination, or will not try;

2. he may call the witness and elicit both the favorable and unfavorable parts of his testimony on direct, thereby taking the sting out of any cross-examination which his adversary may conduct, and hope that the net effect on the jury is, all in all, favorable to his client;

3. he may refuse to call the witness at all, and hope that the opposition does not call him either, or that if it does, he will be able to make more capital for his client by discrediting the witness on cross-examination than the opposition was able to make for its side by drawing out material to its credit.

It will be apparent that the advantage to a litigant in this position is most certainly not to lay all the facts before the court. One consequence of the adversary system as practiced is that if the rules of evidence are manipulated skillfully by the opposing parties, a jury may be asked to reach a decision on a set of very incomplete facts. It is rare that demonstrably false evidence is presented in court in which positively false assertions of fact have been made, but it is common that the jury retires to consider its verdict having heard evidence which has many "holes" in it, because one side or the other of the controversy has managed to exclude from the jury's hearing some significant material. It can be deduced that faced with this state of affairs, witnesses are pawns in the tactician's game, and must be prepared to be used in ways which they did not anticipate and do not like. Their account of the affair that they witnessed may not be asked for except in small and unrepresentative segments, carefully chosen to give a view of what happened that the witness himself does not hold. Since a witness may not generally give his opinion, but only testify to facts, there is no way the jury will find out this is so until after it has delivered its verdict.

All this follows from the desire of litigants to win their cases rather than see justice done--though many litigants delude themselves that the two are synonymous; few legal suitors are wholly on the side of the angels.

Many witnesses have felt, and will no doubt continue to feel, that this is an outrageous state of affairs. They argue, reasonably enough, that the legal process should not compel men to lend their names to an attempted distortion of the facts by the litigants.

It is a form of conscription which may have a witness fighting for one side, while sympathizing with the other. That, however, is the law and there is nothing that a witness can do about it but grin and bear it as best he can. A witness may not choose the side for which he appears. He may dislike the party for whom he appears, may believe that the merits of the action are on the other side and find it thoroughly unpalatable to be called in aid of a scoundrel, but he has no choice in the matter.

The frustrations of a witness are compounded by the fact that often the things which a lawyer wants to adduce from a witness are not co-extensive with what the witness wants to say. Lawyers even have their own adages on this point; one of the most famous is "If a witness wants to be asked a question on cross-examination, don't ask it." Often, a witness makes a great mistake in showing his eagerness to get onto a particular subject: when he does, he shows the opposition that it should not ask about it as clearly as a red light at an intersection tells a driver to stop.

Witness Examination: Question and Answer

The method of the American courts is to obtain information from witnesses by letting the parties question them. The party calling the witness has the first chance to ask questions. This is known as "direct examination" or "examination-in-chief". Then his opponent may question the witness (though he need not) and this is known as "cross-examination". If there has been a cross-examination, the party calling the witness may have another opportunity to question his witness on "re-direct examination". This right to question, and particularly the right to cross-examination, are regarded as fundamental parts of the general right of confrontation: that is, the right to confront one's opponents in court.

The right to confrontation has its origin in criminal proceedings and was at first a rule prohibiting secret accusations. This rule was thought necessary to discourage malicious allegations of crime. It was thought that publicity would reduce the likelihood of ill-founded complaints.

The right of confrontation is regarded as so important that it even overrides the claim of justice to obtain all the information material to a case. This is neatly illustrated by a New York decision, People v. Cole 43 N.Y. 508 (1871), the principle of which is applicable in every state. A lady witness was called by the prosecution in a criminal trial and gave her evidence in response to direct questioning by the district attorney, but before the accused's lawyer had the opportunity to cross-examine her she inexplicably went into convulsions, with the result that the defense never truly obtained its right of confrontation. The unfortunate defendant was convicted, but on appeal his conviction was overturned; the proper course would have been for the trial judge to order the lady's direct testimony to be ignored, or alternatively to recess the trial until she recovered from her convulsions. This decision shows how much the evidence heard by a court depends upon the parties. The practical consequence of the appellate ruling is that the court will be deprived of evidence if one party has been deprived of means of attacking it. A litigant's tactical rights are given priority over the desirability of reaching the truth in any absolute sense.

This tenderness towards the party's rights in litigation and the relative lack of concern it reveals for hearing whatever evidence is available stems from the characteristic of American court procedure that differentiates it from the procedure of most other courts in the world: its adoption of an "adversary" approach and its lack of "inquisitorial" mechanisms. This characteristic is fundamental to the workings of the law in the United States and is the subject of the next chapter.

"Agreed" Facts

There is another way in which the courts can be turned aside from the truth. Although they will not decide points of law on hypothetical facts, in civil cases litigants can "agree" facts in order to avoid the time-consuming process of proving them. When such an agreement is reached it is submitted to the court in advance of, or at the beginning of, trial and the court will assume that the facts were as stated in the agreement between the parties. Such an agreement is known in some jurisdictions as "stipulation" or "submission of undisputed facts". Its advantage is to reduce the expense that the parties would be put to in proving the facts by orthodox means and to minimize the areas of dispute between them. However, it should be noted that the acceptance of these agreements highlights a characteristic of the American legal system which not all authorities believe to be desirable. For it puts the litigants in a position to procure a legal decision on the basis of a misleading set of assumptions about what took place. Since the courts to which such agreements are submitted have no machinery for investigating independently whether the agreed facts are the real ones, or even a close approximation to them, they must rely upon the good faith of the parties to ensure that they are not being offered the chance to pass on a piece of fiction. Two opposing parties could "agree" that a road upon which their traffic accident occurred was 20 feet wide, but it would not alter the fact that it was really 35 feet wide. Agreements between litigants which deliberately mislead the court are probably rare, but the point is that "agreed" facts are not really the truth at all. An agreement of facts made with the ulterior motive of defrauding someone who has an interest in the outcome of litigation even though he is not a party thereto might constitute the crime of conspiring to pervert the course of justice. Attempts to do this are rare, but the temptation exists in cases where an insurance company is standing behind a litigant; both sides may find it advantageous to 'agree'to some important fact so that the insurance company's liability is undisputed. For this reason, among others, most insurance companies insert a term in their policies that gives them the right to be joined as parties in suits where, in effect, they are going to pay any damages awarded.

Chapter VI

THE ADVERSARY PROCEEDING

The legal system of the United States insists that the parties to litigation elicit evidence from witnesses by question and answer and eschews inquisitorial or denunciatory methods. Although these characteristics are most prominently displayed in criminal proceedings, they are to be found in all American trials, criminal and civil.

The method of inquisition has some notoriety as a result of the cruelty of the Spanish Inquisition's attempt to seek out and crush heresy. Actually, the inquisitorial approach to law is perfectly respectable and followed by many civilized countries. Inquisition means that the presiding judge takes a more active role in trial than is usual in the adversary system. He asks the witnesses questions, rather than leaving it to the parties' lawyers. He seeks out the truth as best he can by interrogation, thereby building the record himself. The function of the lawyers in this procedure is to act as watchdogs of their clients' interests, listening carefully to the judge's questions and the answers he receives and correcting any impression created that seems to prejudice their client. On occasion, they may make an offer of proof to the judge, but if it is accepted, he may still take the witness over from the lawyer who evoked his evidence. The inquisitorial system places a great onus on the judge, but in theory is undoubtedly more direct in its attempts to ascertain the truth than the adversary process.

The adversary proceedings which characterize American courts leave the initiative in litigation to the parties and the judge takes a much less prominent role than his counterpart in the inquisitorial system. It is rare for an American judge to ask questions directly of a witness and when he does, it is for the purpose of clarifying a point, or removing an unintentional ambiguity from the record. The rest of the questioning is left to counsel in the case. At every stage, one side has the right to appeal to the judge

36

to prevent a particular line of questions being put by the other side. The judge considers the objection and decides it in most instances at once, though sometimes he will interrupt the trial to hear legal argument on the point, and may even take time to consider. But what is important here, in comparing adversary with inquisitorial rules of court, is that the judge will only consider the point at all if an objection is made by a party. Without an objection being made, there will be no intervention by the judge though he may know perfectly well that the questions being put are against the rules of evidence. That is because in adversary proceedings, it is up to the parties to take the initiative in protecting their rights and the judge will normally intervene only at the application of counsel. Thus, if a prosecutor in a criminal trial forgets to call a material witness, the judge will not remind him to do so but will dismiss the charges against the defendant because, as the Report of the Attorney General's Committee on Poverty and the Administration of Federal Criminal Justice remarked: "the essence of the adversary system is challenge." An exception to the rule of judicial non-intervention is made when a litigant is unrepresented by counsel and therefore not apprised of his rights. In these circumstances, it is understood that the judge has some obligation to act on behalf of the unrepresented party, though judges dislike having to do so, because it puts them in a dual role of judge and advocate.

Perhaps the best description of a judge in the American courts is that he acts as an umpire, but needs nudging. In other words, he will act impartially to protect a party's rights, but only if the party requests his intervention. Inquisitors act on their own initiative and make inquiries regardless of the wishes of the parties. This means that a witness in the American system can look upon the judge as his friend and protector, but must beware of counsel. In inquisitorial proceedings, by contrast, the judge will interrogate a witness, if necessary without mercy, to get at the truth.

Objections to Denunciation

Closely associated with the philosophy of adversary proceedings is the taboo against a witness denouncing the opposition in a speech which includes everything detrimental to it that can be mustered. The objections to this procedure, much used in political trials in some countries, are several and go to the heart of our ideas of justice.

The first objection is that denunciations of this type are irrelevant. It matters not that a litigant is a nasty, even despicable fellow; the issue for the court is whether his claim is lawful. Even bad men have rights!

Second, denunciations do not allow cross-examination to achieve its effect. Even questioning a witness after he had delivered a speech against the opposition is not as effective as the use of the question-and-answer method throughout, because a speech has much more impact in creating an impression (regardless of its truth) than specific answers to questions asked by both sides. The right to cross-examine is a fundamental one, and the use of question-and-answer avoids the possibility that a glib witness will influence the jury by histrionics.

There is, however, another aspect of denunciations which has put them out of favor in this country. If they were permitted, they would have little advantage over the acceptance of a signed statement into evidence, which is rarely done unless the witness is in court at the time, and the signed statement is to be used as a basis for examination. There is a general feeling in the legal community that denunciations, even in the face of the court, can become "set pieces" which conceal the demeanor of the witness much more than the duty to answer questions spontaneously does. A prepared speech of opposition can be rehearsed and polished and its weak points glossed over, but the same cannot be done in preparation for cross-examination. There is much to be learned from the way a witness handles himself on the stand when responding to counsel, whereas a denunciation can be delivered in an artificial way.

The importance of a witness's demeanor on the stand, and the light it throws on his credibility, is much relied upon by appellate courts, which are generally loathe to interfere with findings of fact by a lower court which had the benefit of seeing witnesses, instead of reading a transcript. The classic statement of an appellate tribunal's position in this regard was made by Judge Lamm, of the Supreme Court of Missouri, in Creamer v. Bivert 113 S.W. 1118 (1908), 1120, 1121, who said of a trial judge:

38

"He sees and hears much we cannot see and hear. We well know there are things of pith that cannot be preserved in or shown by the written page of a bill of exceptions. Truth does not always stalk boldly forth naked, but modest withal, in a printed abstract in a court of last resort. She oft hides in nooks and crannies visible only to the mind's eye of the judge who tries the case. To him appears the furtive glance, the blush of conscious shame, the hesitation, the sincere or the flippant or sneering tone, the heat, the calmness, the yawn, the sigh, the candor or lack of it, the scant or full realization of the solemnity of an oath, the carriage and mien. The brazen face of the liar, the glibness of the schooled witness in reciting a lesson, or the itching overeagerness of the swift witness, as well as the honest face of the truthful one, are alone seen by him. In short, one witness may give testimony that reads in print, here, as if falling from the lips of an angel of light, and yet not a soul who heard it, nisi, believed a word of it; and another witness may testify so that it reads brokenly and obscurely in print, and yet there was that about the witness that carried conviction of truth to every soul who heard him testify. Therefore, where an issue in equity rests alone on the credibility of witnesses, the upper court may with entire propriety rest somewhat on the superior advantage of the lower court in determining a fact. "

One other aspect of the rule against speech-making by witnesses deserves mention. There are some matters of which a witness may have knowledge that neither of the parties wishes to bring out in court. Under the question-and-answer method these will not be revealed, because the witness will be given no opportunity to refer to them. He might easily draw them to the court's attention if he was allowed to make a speech, especially if he had "an ax to grind" as some witnesses, like some litigants, undoubtedly do. Thus, a major difference between the two kinds of arrangement for taking legal evidence is this: under the question-and-answer regime, the parties control the facts which come before the court, but where denunciation is permitted the witnesses have it in their power to decide the focus of attention.

On the whole, it is fair to say that a witness has an easier time under the inquisitorial and denunciatory regime common to most civil law countries, because he is spared the rigors of cross-examination. Yet, it should be said in defense of the American common law that a witness is much less likely to find himself in conflict with the judge here. The inquisitor in the civil law is the judge himself, who is capable of as searching a cross-examination as any private attorney will give, and he has no restraints upon him. At common law, the judge remains neutral and can insist that counsel tone down his questioning if it seems unreasonably antagonistic to the witness.

Depositions and Other Written Statements

The right to confront an adverse witness has been considered so important that, on those occasions when it is impracticable that a witness should attend court and a written record of his evidence is made for presentation to the court at an appropriate time, the parties are entitled to go and interview the witness and cross-examine him just as if he was in court. The party who wishes to depose a witness of this sort must serve notice on all other parties when he intends to do so, and they have the right to come along and ask their own questions and object to any they believe inadmissible that the other side asks. Any such objection will be referred to the judge in his chambers for a ruling. What happens when a witness cannot attend court is that, in effect, the court attends him, the only difference being that judge and jury do not visit the witness. Nevertheless, the parties and their counsel act by authority of the court and the witness is sworn in the same way as he would be if he took the stand.

This procedure is most frequently used when the witness is too ill to travel to court, but sometimes it is used to obtain the evidence of a party who could travel, but for reasons other than incapacity should not do so. An example would be a witness who was suffering from a virulently infectious disease, and was being incubated. He might be deposed at the hospital rather than risk a spread of his germs as a consequence of his travelling. Though he might be ready, willing and able to attend court, the court might not be ready to receive him!

It is the widespread belief of the legal profession that depositions are not as satisfactory a way of obtaining testimony as the conventional method of subpoenaing a witness to attend court. Neither the judge nor the jury (if any) has a chance to see what kind of person the witness is and make an assessment of his trustworthiness. All they have to go by is the transcription of what is said when he was deposed, which is a cold, inhuman substitute for seeing the man himself. For this reason, the courts are reluctant to authorize depositions if there is any prospect of getting the witnesses before them.

This objection to depositions has even greater force when applied to the submission of a narrative written statement by a witness. Additionally, this kind of statement may not cover all the matters that the parties regard as pertinent and without the presence of the person who executed the statement they cannot be explored. Yet, if he is to be there in case of this contingency, he might just as well be put on the stand in the normal way.

In practice, American courts never accept written statements made by persons still living as evidence of the truth of what is stated. However, they are widely used for the purpose of showing inconsistency between a witness's recollection at the time he made the written statement and his later recollection at the time he gives evidence from the stand.

The Right to Question a Witness

The right to question a witness in open court is not, of course, a totally unrestricted one. The parties must confine themselves to matters that are relevant and admissible according to the law of evidence. The standard by which questions are judged is whether they are designed to elicit an answer of which as a matter of law the court can make use. This leads to the paradoxical position that a court decides whether a question ought to be allowed to be asked by its prediction of the response it will probably elicit. It does sometimes happen that the court deliberates long and hard over admissibility on a premise that the answer will be of a certain type, when the witness concerned, who is all the time standing by, knows that the answer he will give will be quite different from what is expected! Questions of admissibility are decided outside the presence of the jury, so as to avoid prejudicing the party who is requesting that a question be ruled inadmissible.

The rules of evidence are some of the most technical parts of the law and a witness may be thankful that he is not expected to know them. However, they may be said to have two primary purposes:

1. to strike a balance between the courts' desire to hear the truth and its desire to keep out of the jury's hands matter that is prejudicial, inflammatory or untrustworthy, and

2. to achieve relevance, so that the parties are not able to introduce matter of no, or little value to the court.

In furtherance of the second aim, the law will only receive evidence of a fact in issue, or a fact material to an issue. This is much easier stated than explained, but an example will ease our path. Suppose the law provides that a will is valid only if in due form, prescribed by statute. Aunt Agnes dies leaving a will in due form which bequeathes all her property to her nephew Tom. Agnes's son George is disgruntled that he was left nothing, and seeks to challenge Tom's inheritance. He asks the court before which his case is brought to allow him to bring evidence that Agnes really meant to destroy the will before she died, and had expressed an intention to him that he should inherit instead of Tom. In these circumstances, the fact in issue is whether the will is valid; if so, Tom inherits. It will be a fact material to that issue of Agnes did anything to invalidate it after it was made. It will be immaterial that she told George she really intended him to inherit, because the law does not recognize oral wills; they must be in due form, prescribed by statute. Thus, George will not be permitted to bring evidence that Agnes did indeed tell him that. George may have ten prospective witnesses lined up outside the courtroom, who will swear that Agnes said George should have her property, but the judge will not allow them to approach the stand. Proof of that fact will do no good, since it will not influence the court's decision.

In practice, the examples which come before the courts are nearly always more complicated than this, for the good reason that lawyers usually foresee and avoid the sort of disappointment that George would experience prior to trial and drop such a hopeless claim. But the principle is sound, and it is precisely this sort of disappointment that leads an optimistic lawyer to subpoena witnesses whom the judge may never allow to be heard.

This example contemplates a ruling by the court which will completely prohibit the witness from appearing, because he has nothing to tell which can influence the court's decision. But the commoner situation is that a witness is permitted to testify, but only to certain matters and he is stopped from telling all he knows for one reason or another. Some of the considerations that guide all courts are that:

1. a witness must testify only to things of which he has personal knowledge. He must not pass on second-hand gossip, or hearsay;

2. a witness may not give his opinion, but only facts, unless he is qualified as an "expert";

3. a witness comes before the court as a servant of justice, not a servant of his own ends. From this it follows that he may not try to engage the court's attention upon his own stake in the proceedings. This applies even if the witness is also a party; when he is on the stand, his interest is irrelevant. His testimony is heard solely for the aid of the court, and as a witness he is not permitted to take the opportunity to plead his case. That can be done at the close of the case by his lawyer, or himself if he appears without counsel.

Of course, a witness is not supposed to try to make up for the deficiencies of counsel in the case. There are many questions which go unanswered in litigation because they have never been asked. A witness who knows the answer to these questions should not try to give them anyway, even though they have not been put. His best procedure is to give answers to those questions he is asked in a way that is short, direct and to the point. If further information is needed, counsel (or, occasionally, the judge) can ask another question, but unless they do, a witness should remain silent and not try to "second guess" the court. A witness is rarely in a position to know whether a question has been omitted because of oversight or for some good and sufficient legal or strategic reason and he is unfairly usurping the prerogative of the parties if he tries to impose his additional knowledge on the court without invitation. He must learn the art characterized by one writer as "the knack of answering only what he was asked."

Sometimes, a witness is desperately anxious to be asked a particular question, either because it reflects credit on him, or he considers it an important one. What can he do if the question is never asked? The answer is that he can do nothing; he is there only to answer the questions put, and no more. What he thinks is relevant is irrelevant. Many a witness has left the stand thinking ruefully "If only I had been asked . . . ." Careful reflection will show that really this is a sensible rule of procedure. Witnesses might flounder about unnecessarily wasting time if they were given free rein to say what they believed to be germane.

It is difficult to lay down any hard-and-fast rule about how fully a witness is entitled to answer a question once it has been posed. It is irritating to a witness to embark on an answer and then be abruptly cut off by counsel halfway through, and the more courageous witnesses appeal to the judge to allow them to "finish their answers", a request which may or may not be granted. The decision depends on whether the answer seems to be relevant and, of course, relevance is a matter of degree. The best way of avoiding clashes with counsel of this kind is to keep answers very short, giving simple "yes" or "no" responses to any questions that can fairly be answered so. It can be taken as a general proposition that if a witness finds himself intending to answer a question lengthily, he is probably attempting an answer much fuller than is wanted and running the risk of being cut off. There are few people who can answer a simple question simply in any circumstances, but their inability grows as they conscientiously consider the matter on the witness stand. The question: "Was it raining on Tuesday?" is not an invitation to digress on the general state of the weather, though many witnesses take it to be. This is answerable by "yes" or "no". If the answer is "yes", it may be permissible to add an adverb like "slightly" or "heavily", but if a witness is intent on avoiding controversy he should not tack on these descriptions, even if they are appropriate. Counsel can ask another question to adduce how hard it was raining; this is an example of the knack of answering only what is asked.

There is one further difficulty that a prospective witness may wish to have cleared up. Witnesses are frequently asked questions by counsel to which the other side objects. Should the witness answer the question at once, or should he wait until the judge has ruled whether the question is admissible or not? A wise witness

44

will wait and see how the judge rules, if the objection is made before he has answered. On the other hand, he does nothing wrong in answering before objection is made, even if he thinks that opposition attorneys are about to object. The speed with which they do so is their worry; the witness is not presumed to be an expert on the law of evidence, or to take responsibility for the propriety of the lawyers' conduct. When this happens, the judge will decide whether the question was admissible without regard to the answer, if any, that the witness gave. If he decides that the question was inadmissible he will direct the jury to ignore the answer. This is legally sufficient to prevent a mistrial being declared, even though it is extremely dubious that a jury does ignore what it hears merely because it is told to. A famous trial lawyer, Clarence Darrow, wrote:

> "Few judges are psychologists, or they would re-
> alize that nothing can be stricken out of a human
> consciousness after being once let in. Judges
> seem to be quite unaware that it is a hard task
> to put anything into the average mind, and, once
> in, an impossible one to take it out."

This comment is a little unfair; many judges realize that a direction to ignore a piece of inadmissible evidence is ineffective, but they give these directions because they are the best tool available to attempt to right the wrong. The law could not be administered if every inadmissible question and answer that were let into a case aborted the proceedings; no trial is ever perfect. When inadmissible testimony creeps in, however, the witness is the least blameworthy of all those involved in the trial and he may privately give thanks that it is not his lot to ponder the complexities of the law of evidence. On the other hand, it is quite improper for a witness to answer a question after the judge has ruled it inadmissible. As happened in the first trial of Alger Hiss, a witness who does this lays himself open to charges of contempt.

As suggested in the previous chapter, the law has a special and restrictive definition of "the truth". It follows from this that a witness who has done what he is bidden, and submitted himself to examination by the parties, has discharged his duty. How far his literal answers and actuality coincide will depend partly on the skill with which the questions are put and partly on the witness's inclination to aid counsel by giving full answers. Consciously or not, most witnesses end up by taking sides and looking on one side as good and the other bad. It is a natural attitude, encouraged by the adversary nature of the proceedings in Anglo-American courts and most witnesses probably try rather harder to aid one side than the other. This help comes not from dishonesty, but from "trimming" testimony so that it paints a picture more useful to one litigant than to his rival. This is often done simply as a favor to the side that gains, without any expectation of advantage by the witness; he has become emotionally involved in the outcome of the litigation.

The borderline between this type of bias in a witness and actively misleading a court is a difficult one to pinpoint, and no number of abstract principles can provide a formula for good faith. But a witness whose feelings are running high about a case in which he is called to appear should guard against distorting the truth to the advantage of one side or the other. After all, it is the court that should decide the merits of the action, not the witnesses.

Chapter VII

KEEPING WITNESSES HONEST

The law can only be fairly applied if witnesses tell the truth--
and throughout history courts have done their best to discourage
dishonesty. Some of the means favored for this purpose in the
past strike us today as odd. The ancient Greeks, for example,
would only allow slaves to testify under torture, the theory being
that slaves were naturally mendacious and would only tell the truth
under duress.

The present law tries to assure the honesty of witnesses by
making them swear to tell the truth, by making perjury an offense,
by giving witnesses protection from interference by third parties,
if necessary and by prohibiting others from interfering with prospective witnesses by threats, by inciting perjury, or bribery. In
spite of these laws, there is little that the law can do to prevent
untruthfulness by a determined and clever liar. District attorneys
often find themselves confronted with alibis that they have substantial reason to doubt, but they have no hope of proving perjured,
because the story has been molded so that it is impossible to disprove and because, as mentioned later in this chapter, the burden
of proof in perjury cases is particularly heavy. In practice the
courts have to presume that most witnesses are truthful.

Of course, the presumption of truthfulness can easily be overturned if facts appear that make it inappropriate and it is particularly weak where a person with a strong interest in the proceedings is testifying to his own advantage. Two hundred years ago,
legal opinion was that the chances of getting the truth out of a witness in these circumstances were so poor that it was better not
to let him testify at all, and so people with an interest in the result
of litigation were not allowed to testify. Today, they may testify
like anybody else, and their credibility is for the jury to decide.

One way to decrease the chances of perjury would be to prevent a witness from testifying to anything which by its nature was
impossible to disprove. For example, if X had been called to

47

testify that, just before Y died, they had both been out walking together on a deserted seashore and Y had given him all his personal property, such testimony would be inadmissible because there would be no way of proving it true or false. On the other hand, if X intended to testify that Z came along with them and overheard Y's gift to X, that would be admissible providing that Z were still alive. The trouble with such a rule is that although it does decrease the risk of perjury it also decreases the possibility that the courts will hear the truth as well. Notwithstanding this objection, there are laws based upon this principle of exclusion known as "dead man statutes".

The assumption that a witness will tell the truth is not unique to courts of law. On the contrary, it is part of our culture that most statements--spoken or written--are taken to be true. Generally, when we see a signpost telling us that a highway will take us to Chicago we believe it without question. But whereas a liar in everyday life suffers no special consequences from his lying (unless he finally becomes notorious for dishonesty), the courts impose special sanctions on him if they discover he is lying by prosecuting for perjury. An essential ingredient of that offense, however, is that the witness has taken an oath to tell the truth, an important circumstance that distinguishes him from an "everyday" liar.

The Oath

Witnesses in all judicial proceedings are required to make a formal declaration before the court that they are telling the truth. In most cases, this will be an oath of which the usual form is: "I swear to tell the truth, the whole truth, and nothing but the truth, so help me God." However, those people who have religious objections to taking an oath are permitted to affirm.

The purpose of making witnesses swear to the truthfulness of their testimony was originally to invoke God's wrath upon a liar. Today, oaths are retained to impress witnesses with the solemnity of their obligation to tell the truth and because the crime of perjury is defined so that a prosecutor must show that an accused made his allegedly false statements after being sworn. A refusal by a witness to give a court an undertaking to tell the truth amounts to contempt because it prevents the witness from being heard at all; unsworn testimony is not admissible.

There are two well-established exceptions to the general rule that a witness must swear an oath before he can be heard. A person accused of crime may elect to make an unsworn statement on his own behalf instead of swearing the oath and taking the witness stand in the normal way. The right to make a statement of this kind is a common law right established when a defendant was barred from giving evidence as a witness because his interest in the outcome was too great for him to be reliable. As a kind of consolation to the accused, the practice grew up of allowing him to say whatever he wished from "the dock", which was the part of the court where a defendant had to stay during his trial. He could say what he liked in his own defense or exoneration, and could not be cross-examined, because he was not a witness in the true sense. He was not sworn because it was thought displeasing to God to put a man on oath who had manifest incentives to lie. No matter how preposterous his statement was, he could not be prosecuted for perjury since he was unsworn.

The other exception deals with children, who are sometimes allowed to testify if the judge is satisfied of his or her ability to understand the obligation to speak the truth. (See Michigan's Revised Judicature Act, 1961, section 2163.) Children are not sworn below a certain age because it is felt not to be proper to put them through a solemn oath that they may not truly understand.

It should be noted that the words of the oath do not hold a witness responsible if the net effect of his testimony is misleading, even though it is truthful. Since a witness cannot tell all he knows, but can only answer questions as they are put to him by the judge or counsel, the total impression of what he says is outside his control. The adversary nature of American trial proceedings makes it attractive to counsel on either side to draw only parts of a witness's knowledge out of him, leaving the aspects of the case less helpful to their clients unrevealed. A result of this method of procedure can be suggestio falsi, suppressio veri (i.e. that a false inference will be invited by failing to state all the material facts), for which the witness has no answerability. This use of witnesses is characteristic and exemplifies a wider principle of the law that they should be given almost no choice about their part in a trial: for just as they cannot choose what they tell a court, they cannot choose whether to appear or not, for they are compellable and neither can they choose on which side of a case they appear, for normally either side is entitled to call any witness it likes. This aspect of a witness's position will be adverted to later.

A few states (such as California: see its Evidence Code, section 700-01) have blanket provisions disqualifying witnesses who are incapable of understanding the duty to tell the truth, even though there is no contention that they are insane, or mentally ill. Doubts about such capability are usually raised before the oath is administered.

Perjury

Perjury has always been regarded as a most serious offense against justice both because it is done in the face of the court and because it poisons the stream of evidence. It is committed by a witness who intentionally, under oath, makes a false statement regarding a material fact. Some witnesses are worried that they may commit perjury "by mistake"; but it will be seen that this is an impossibility, because perjury can only be committed intentionally--an honest mistake while testifying is no crime and does not render a witness liable to any penalty whatsoever.

There are very few prosecutions for perjury even though many observers believe that it is common. The reason for the paucity of prosecutions is that special onerous burdens of proof have been imposed on the prosecutor of this crime, the major examples of which are known as the "two witness rule" and the "direct evidence rule". These rules were disapproved by the President's Commission on Law Enforcement and the Administration of Justice which concluded that in methods of proof: "there is no apparent reason for the distinction between perjury and other crimes."

Perjury involves a false statement, knowingly made, about a material fact, a lie about a matter which is not likely to influence the proceedings is not sufficient.

Nowadays the penalty for perjury (which is in all jurisdictions severe) is laid down in the relevant statute, but in bygone ages a perjurer was punished in several different ways. For instance, William Penn's Frame of Government, applied to Pennsylvania in 1682, provided that any person found guilty of perjury "shall suffer and undergo such damage or penalty, as the person, or persons, against whom he or she bore false witness, did, or should, undergo; and shall also make satisfaction to the party wronged, and be publicly exposed as a false witness, never to be credited in any court, or before any Magistrate . . . ." The laws of a few states still follow William Penn's example so far as disqualification of a convicted perjurer from testifying in any subsequent proceedings, but the modern approach is to let perjurers testify and leave the jury to assess their credibility. There is also a possibility that to render a perjurer incompetent ever to testify again is a cruel and unusual punishment and hence unconstitutional under the Eighth Amendment.

Interference with Witnesses

At common law, it was an offense to "suborn" perjury--that is, to encourage someone to commit it. However, most states have dropped subornation of perjury as a separate crime and prosecute under more general provisions outlawing solicitation or incitement of any crime. The offense, whether it is called subornation, incitement or solicitation of perjury is committed whether or not perjury resulted; the gravamen of the crime rests in trying to get perjury committed, successfully or not.

A special form of subornation is bribery of a witness which is often a distinct crime under state criminal codes. The essence of the crime here is not the paying of, or offer to pay a witness (because this is not unlawful and indeed is commonly practiced with expert witnesses), but paying with the intention of influencing the substance of what a witness will say under oath. Again, it does not matter whether the intention is fulfilled. Some statutes define bribery widely so that it is not confined to an offer of money. For example, the Connecticut Penal Code, section 151 provides that "A person is guilty of bribery of a witness if he offers, confers, or agrees to confer upon a witness any benefit to influence the testimony or conduct of such witness . . . ." "Benefit" means gain or advantage, or anything regarded by the beneficiary as a gain or advantage, including benefit to any person or entity in whose welfare he is interested. Under this kind of provision, the offense would be committed if a prospective witness was offered an expense-paid vacation with his mother-in-law provided that he regarded it as a benefit to himself, or a benefit to his mother-in-law if it could be shown that he was interested in his mother-in-law's welfare.

A corollary to the prohibition of bribery is the prohibition of intimidation or threatening of a person called as a witness. Generally, intimidation is defined as an intention to place someone in fear of injury or reprisal. Some states impose a specially high penalty for threatening a witness. A witness who is threatened should report the matter at once to the police; he is entitled to round-the-clock protection if the circumstances warrant it.

The fear of reprisal can be particularly well-founded in litigation which involves organized criminal activity, a matter which was studied by the President's Commission on Law Enforcement and Administration of Justice, which reported:

> "No jurisdiction has made adequate provision for protecting witnesses in organized crime cases from reprisal. In the few instances where guards are provided, resources require their withdrawal shortly after the particular trial terminates. On a case-to-case basis, governments have helped witnesses find jobs in other sections of the country or have even helped them emigrate. The difficulty of obtaining witnesses because of the fear of reprisal could be countered somewhat if governments had established systems for protecting cooperative witnesses.

> "The Federal Government should establish residential facilities for the protection of witnesses desiring such assistance during the pendency of organized crime litigation.

> "After trial, the witness should be permitted to remain at the facility so long as he needs to be protected. The Federal Government should establish regular procedures to help Federal and local witnesses who fear organized crime reprisal, to find jobs and places to live in other parts of the country, and to preserve their anonymity from organized crime groups."

It is a sad commentary on the state of the nation that the Commission was forced to recognize that some witnesses needed residential protection from reprisal and indeed, might have to forge a new identity to ensure their safety.

A witness who is in fear of attack as a result of his testimony, or intended testimony, should ask for protection at the earliest opportunity. In any case where there is a reasonable apprehension of violence, there is a duty on the public authorities to provide a bodyguard. The trouble is that this duty is not an enforceable one by the person in danger, and a witness has no right to demand protection additional to the normal police protection that every citizen receives. The judgment as to whether extraordinary measures are required is in the hands of the authorities.

In many states, threats of physical injury are themselves crimes and will be actively investigated by the police. In addition, some states make tampering with a witness a separate offense. Section 153 of the Connecticut Penal Code, for example, provides:

> "A person is guilty of tampering with a witness if, believing that an official proceeding is pending or about to be instituted, he induces or attempts to induce a witness to testify falsely, withhold testimony, elude legal process summoning him to testify or absent himself from any official proceeding."

The inducement may be by bribe, or threat, or other means and the offense is classified as a felony. Unpleasantness of this kind is rare in civil cases, though it does occasionally surface where feelings run high. Interference with a witness is an attempt to pervert the course of justice and as such is treated with severity when discovered. Nearly all the offenses which can be committed in respect of witnesses are also prosecutable under general provisions forbidding obstruction or perversion of the course of justice.

A threat to prosecute a witness criminally, or an offer to refrain from his prosecution, made with a view to obtaining advantageous testimony from him in a civil case is a breach of legal ethics, even if there is good cause for believing that the witness would be convicted if prosecuted. That seems to be the result of Disciplinary Rule 7-105 of the A.B.A.'s Code of Professional

Responsibility which states that a lawyer must not threaten to present criminal charges solely to obtain an advantage in a civil matter. The weakness of this provision is that the threat may not be made "solely" for that reason, but may also partially be motivated by a sense of public duty to stifle crime.

Chapter VIII

BEHAVIOR IN COURT

The pomp and ceremony of a court should not encourage a witness to behave unnaturally while giving testimony. The best course is to be oneself; courts are used to seeing a motley parade of humanity and will forgive many foibles. A witness makes a mistake by pretending to be something he is not, or putting on airs, or assuming a manner of speech that he does not normally use, or feigning a sophistication he does not possess.

Of course, there are limits to the advice to act naturally. A lady in New London, Connecticut, who decided that a court was a suitable place to strip naked was given a jail sentence of thirty days for contempt by an astounded judge. In general, it is best to remain fairly passive in court, speaking only when spoken to, and not embarking upon even small enterprises of one's own such as combing one's hair, or entering a private conversation while the court is in session, let alone taking off one's clothes. There is a general duty of respect to any court and gratuitous misconduct in its face will almost certainly bring sanctions in its wake. The possible sorts of misconduct are infinitely varied, but among them might be cited cursing, unruliness, deliberate attempts to disrupt the proceedings, appearing drunk or under the influence of drugs, threatening any court official, swearing, making obscene or distracting gestures, smoking, spitting and chewing gum. A judge has a wider power to control conduct in his court than a policeman has to control conduct on the street and he can insist on observance of standards of "good taste" as well as observance of the law by those in his court. In this respect, a judge in his court is like a homeowner in his home; to a large extent he can set whatever rules he pleases for the conduct of those present. Whatever the private feelings a witness may have about the proceedings, his wise course will be an outward display of deference.

The judge has the ultimate power to commit an unruly witness for contempt, though that is a power rarely exercised without warning. Generally, a judge will content himself with admonishing an unruly witness to begin with, and only resort to the threat of punishment for contempt after severe provocation and several prior requests to the witness to improve his conduct. Often, a witness becomes belligerent on the stand not because he has any grievance against the judge, but because he feels he has been taunted and annoyed by counsel for one of the parties. Here, the judge is in a difficult position. He may personally sympathize with the anger shown by a witness who is being roughly treated by counsel, yet feel that in the circumstances he can do nothing to tone down the grilling that the witness is experiencing; there are occasions when the interests of justice are not best served by showing tenderness towards witnesses. Even where it appears to the judge that a witness is receiving more buffeting than need be from an attorney, he will be reluctant to intervene. Many witnesses do not understand why this should be.

The first fear a judge has is that his interference in examination of a witness will become a ground for appeal. Second, his powers over lawyers tend to be somewhat less than his powers over lay members of the public, because lawyers will be rather less impressed by the majesty of a judge's office and also because their paramount duty is to their clients, not the judge. A request from the judge to tone down their cross-examination may not impress them much when they know that their conduct is nothing that could amount to contempt. It has always been a tricky matter to know just what a lawyer may or may not do in cross-examination, especially as a by-product of the adversary system, when witnesses unconsciously take sides. The Canons of Professional Ethics drawn up by the American Bar Association, which for many years represented its official policy on professional conduct, provided:

> "A lawyer should always treat adverse witnesses
> and suitors with fairness and due consideration,
> and he should never minister to the malevolence
> or prejudices of a client in the trial or conduct
> of a case."

However, on January 1, 1970, the Canons were superseded by a new "Code of Professional Responsibility" in which the provision of the Canons quoted above was not repeated, or indeed replaced by any equivalent language. This omission is interesting, in that it provides indirect evidence of how vexing a question a lawyer's conduct towards witnesses can be. This is especially highlighted by a reference to the Canons of Judicial Ethics, drawn up by the same body, exhorting judges to be considerate of witnesses (Canon 9) and require and enforce on the part of clerks, court officers and counsel civility and courtesy to witnesses (Canon 10). A comparison of the provisions of the Canons of Professional Ethics and Judicial Ethics show that A.B.A. regards the duty of courtesy as a different one for a lawyer than for a judge. In recognition of this a judge is told to enforce civility and courtesy, whereas a lawyer is told only to be fair and show "due consideration". Of course, opinions can and do differ as to the consideration that ought to be shown particular witnesses. Certainly, the demeanor of most lawyers in cross-examining a witness is not what is normally called courtesy. The Canons drawn up by the A.B.A. have no authority in law, but only represent the thinking of those members of the legal profession who have joined it and endorsed its aims, and as such they serve to highlight some of the difficulties in laying down rules of conduct for lawyers and witnesses alike.

The conclusion that a sensible witness will draw from this is that the best way to regulate his exchanges on cross-examination is by the exercise of self-restraint, and an absolute refusal to lose his temper, even in the face of provocation. Some people who regularly have to take the stand in the course of their duties --forensic experts, policemen and the like--put a note to themselves in their pockets, reminding them to keep calm. The fact is that in court, as elsewhere, it takes two to quarrel and if one refuses to be drawn into fight, the temperature is considerably lowered. It is the regrettable technique of some counsel to try to provoke a witness so that he appears uncontrolled and vindictive to the jury, and this is a special reason for keeping a tight watch over what one says. By far the best manner of answering all questions, no matter how provocative they are, is an open, serious response that displays no particular emotion. There will be occasions when emotion is understandable, but it should relate to the events being referred to, and not to the witness's feeling about counsel.

The potential for heated exchanges with counsel is especially great when a witness feels that he has been called to aid the "wrong" side--that is, the side with which he feels no sympathy. A witness in these circumstances objects not to the legal proceedings themselves, but the use to which he is put. The law brands witnesses of this persuasion "hostile witnesses". There are several special rules relating to hostile witnesses, the most important of them being that the party which calls a witness who is designated hostile can cross-examine him. This is an exception to the general rule that a party can only cross-examine the other side's witnesses. The unwillingness of a witness to aid a party of whom he disapproves is no excuse in law for withholding his testimony, and an attempt to do so is punishable as contempt.

There are two techniques beloved of some trial counsel which are an attempt to maximize the impact of a favorable answer from a witness that, though strictly unethical, are very rarely disciplined unless they are repeated so much that the judge feels compelled to intervene. The first is to ask a question that is clearly inadmissible, in the hope that a witness will answer it before the other side has time to object. Naturally, these questions are always of the sort that are likely to elicit an answer that will aid the questioning party's case. Although, as explained earlier, the judge will direct the jury to ignore tha answer to such a question, it is somewhat unrealistic to expect the jury to blot out entirely what they have heard. In this way, counsel hopes to get the best of both worlds: to draw attention to material that may help his client while avoiding having to introduce it formally into evidence.

There are limits to this technique: for instance, if prosecuting counsel in a criminal trial tried to slip the fact that the defendant had previous convictions into the jury's knowledge in this way, it would be a ground for declaring a mistrial. But in less blatant instances, judges usually content themselves with merely reprimanding counsel and instructing the jury to put the inadmissible facts out of their minds. A witness cannot do much to avoid being exploited this way and is not responsible to the court if he answers such a question, since he is not expected to know the rules of evidence and unless otherwise directed, must answer all questions put to him by counsel for the respective sides. He should not try to anticipate objections, thereby arrogating the job of the lawyers to himself.

The other technique to be seen in this light is the pretense of counsel not to have heard a reply given on cross-examination which is important to his client. Here, there is no doubt that the question and hence the answer elicited are admissible, but counsel affects to mishear so that the witness repeats himself and the jury has the second opportunity to let the fact sink in. In strict law, repetitive questions are inadmissible, so that counsel must accept the answer to a question that a witness first gave; the witness is on oath and therefore is presumed to tell the truth on a given fact at the first opportunity. Repetition of a question, or a request to repeat an answer, is tantamount to giving a witness a chance to modify his previous statement, which he should not do.

Although a witness will probably come across these two tactics in any long trial, and especially if he is subpoenaed to proceedings of a criminal nature, they are a double-edged benefit to a lawyer's client. Juries sometimes realize that the lawyer is "pulling a fast one" and resent it. Furthermore, what one side can do, so can the other and if a judge has seen this kind of thing working to the benefit of one party, he will be disinclined to prevent at least an equal number of occurrences for the other side. It should be said in fairness that sometimes repetition is not deliberate; counsel have many things on their minds during the course of a trial and may completely innocently go over the same ground again and, of course, may genuinely mishear a witness. In a major criminal trial in New York City, the defense misheard a prosecution witness who said "my life was in great danger in New York City" and thought he said "my wife was in great danger...." to the considerable embarrassment and puzzlement of the court and his client. This possibility of misunderstanding is high in some courts, because their acoustics leave much to be desired and they are continually the victims of noise, as court officials and members of the public enter and leave. Some courts are not equipped with microphones and so the audibility of a witness depends on the strength of his delivery.

A witness should always try to speak clearly, articulating his words properly and pitching his voice at a louder level than he uses for normal conversation. Some witnesses, being self-conscious, speak much too softly, to the distress of judge and jury alike. There is no shame in addressing a court and a witness should aim to make himself heard. He should face the person questioning him directly, and not look downwards, or appear to be avoiding the gaze of lawyer, client or jury. To do so creates an impression that he is evasive, though the true explanation is usually modesty bred of embarrassment. Most witnesses find that they become progressively more at ease while on the witness stand, but everyone should try to put a bold face on from the beginning.

Some witnesses have a special reason for being timorous, because they have an informity or disability. It is always best to forewarn the court of this, because even the most imposing lawyer will show consideration for a disabled person.

There are two personal problems which witnesses are often most worried about. One of them is a tendency to stutter. This is a nervous complaint, like asthma, and if counsel know of a witness's difficulty in advance, they will readily make special allowance for it; even lawyers are human. The other is incontinence which is serious enough to require a witness to make frequent visits to the rest room, especially when he is under stress. A witness who will be on the stand for some time who suffers this affliction is often most worried about this problem. If it is revealed privately to the lawyer who calls him, an arrangement can often be made with the judge that an adjournment will be called by the judge at a given signal from the witness. The infirmity will be treated confidentially and the signal can be pre-agreed and unobstrusive so that no one in the courtroom will know, except those let into the secret. Of course, witnesses who are crippled, or must use appliances to get around because of illness or accident will always be given special facilities.

Jurors, as arbiters of fact, are the judges of a witness's credibility, and there is reason to suppose that they take account of a witness's appearance, just as everyone takes account of appearance. A witness who is undecided what to wear, or how to look, should err on the side of conservatism. Neat, clean and respectable witnesses fare best because they are the ones that the bulk of jurors find easiest to identify with. Male witnesses have an easier choice than females, because they can safely appear wearing a suit, or the uniform of their occupations. The range of dress acceptable for a woman is much broader, but it is best to bend towards formality and to avoid ostentation (such as expensive jewelry) or flashiness. Dark glasses should not be worn on the stand and witnesses who do so without good medical reason will probably be asked to remove them, on the ground they they impede the jury's view of a witness's expression.

The nuances of demeanor are believed to be revealing of character by many people, but the difficulty is to agree what significance particular habits and poses have. The courts do not inquire into the inferences that a jury draws from a witness's behavior while facing the court, but it is acknowledged that the jury is entitled to come to its own conclusions as to credibility. These conclusions may be quite unscientific and are one of the mysteries of jury trial.

However, before a jury retires to consider its findings, it will be instructed on questions of credibility by the judge. These instructions will tell the jurors what they may and may not decide to be significant and contain snippets of evidentiary law to guide them. However, there is no way in which the judge (or anyone else) can ensure that these guidelines are followed because jury deliberations are secret and only inquired into in the most exceptional circumstances. A wily jury could therefore make findings which cut completely across the legal instructions delivered to them by the judge and no one could do anything about it. A decision against the weight of the evidence is virtually invulnerable, providing that it is not one that it was impossible for the jury to come to on the evidence presented to them. This is especially true in criminal trials where the jury delivers an unexpected acquittal, because the prosecution has no right of appeal. One of the factors upon which a jury has most freedom is in deciding whether to accept or reject the testimony of a given witness.

In law, every witness must be accepted on his merits. There is no class of witness to which the law accords a special presumption of credibility. This means that a jury is as free to find a clergyman to be a liar as it is to believe a used-car salesman; each witness is assessed individually. Nevertheless, there are certain types of witness of whom the jury may be warned if their interest, or bias, is a strong one. For instance, an accomplice in a criminal case who gives evidence against a co-accused has a strong incentive to throw all the blame on him and the jury may be so warned. Similarly, the claimants in a will dispute have a direct interest in diverting the decedent's property to themselves.

Then again, there are certain types of witness whom the jury may conclude to be suspect without any prompting from the law. On this ground, an experienced trial lawyer deprecated the value of a mother's testimony on behalf of a child who was in trouble. "A mother's alibi isn't worth much, " he said. "Let me tell you something: I have a mother, you have a mother, policemen have mothers, judges have mothers, animals in the jungle have mothers --even snakes have mothers. " The common law thought it so likely that a spouse would stick up for his mate that it made him incompetent to testify, a partial disability that still persists in some states.

The other criterion of credibility that a jury uses is whether a witness's story is inherently unlikely. It would take a lot to convince a jury that a witness had seen the Empire State Building move two blocks, though he might be an honest individual of impeccable reputation. Here, too, the judgment is highly subjective, because just as the credibility of witnesses varies, so does the credulity of jurors.

Chapter IX

THE REPUTATION OF WITNESSES

It is said that there are few citizens who participate in a lawsuit who come out of it with a better reputation than the one with which they went in. The law can be cruel in exposing long-buried secrets and holding up to public view many things which had previously been hidden. For this reason alone, many prospective witnesses would prefer not to have to enter the courtroom, but the long arm of the law can usually reach out and compel them.

Before considering the ways in which a witness may find attempts being made to impeach his reputation, it is worth noting that some prospective witnesses wish to avoid testifying for honorable reasons that have nothing to do with a desire to avoid the possibility that their characters will be besmirched. A witness may feel the lawsuit inappropriate. Perhaps the most common reason is that he believes that the circumstances are such that they will not justify legal intervention, and any dispute that has arisen will be better dealt with by informal, extra-legal means. Examples are frequently found in the administration of the criminal law, where in the heat of the moment someone has complained to the police, or the district attorney's office and after he has calmed down, regretted that officialdom has been brought into the matter at all. Two instances are provided by complaints of assault and complaints of rape (or lesser sexual attacks). The complainant in this kind of case quite frequently regrets that the legal machinery has been set in motion, especially when (as happens in many cases) the alleged assailant is known personally to the complainant. After the event it may seem that the conduct complained of was reasonable, or at least excusable and that it would be better for everyone concerned if the incident were forgotten. Nevertheless, the authorities may press charges although the complainant, who will be the principal witness in a resulting prosecution, does not wish them to be pressed. Where this happens, a complainant who has been duly subpoenaed must give evidence, or face conviction for contempt. Most district attorneys' offices will drop charges if a complaint is withdrawn, but some do not. The important thing is that the case has, in a sense, become the property of the office once a formal allegation of crime has been received.

A different rule prevails in civil proceedings, because they can be terminated by a private individual. Where a family matter is referred to the courts because of dissension among the relatives, it can always be withdrawn by agreement and no one will then be subpoenaed to testify. Withdrawals of this kind generally require the approval of a judge, but it is willingly given in nearly all cases.

A witness giving important evidence against the claim of a party to litigation may find that, although that party produces no direct evidence to contradict him, he is attacked for his credibility. This attack will take the form of an attack on his reputation, his character and his reliability and can often lead to embarrassing confrontation for a witness with skeletons in the closet. A witness takes the risk of having the other side try to discredit him publicly and should be prepared for it. In recent years, much has been made of the so-called "right to privacy" seen by some in Constitutional provisions and recognized to exist by the Supreme Court in several notable decisions, but the right does little for a witness whose past and psyche are pored over in open court in an effort to persuade the jury that he is not to be believed. The law is no respecter of persons, or persons' feelings if they happen to be witnesses under cross-examination. Anyone who has been subpoenaed should be forewarned of the possible ways in which an attempt at impeachment may be made. "Impeachment" is a legal term which all too frequently can be a substitute for "character assassination".

A first, and direct, way of impeaching a witness is to show that his past is not blameless. He can be confronted with his record in open court and asked how he explains the less savory parts of it. Matters such as a past bankruptcy, or an unpleasant divorce, or a discharge from employment can be admissible in this context. Apart from this, a witness's previous convictions for crime are normally always adducable in evidence. This comes as a surprise to many people, who think that there is a rule against using this material. It is true, there is a rule; but it applies only to criminally accused persons, whose past convictions may not be drawn to the attention of the jury by prosecuting counsel, except in most unusual circumstances. But an ordinary witness is not protected from his past in this manner--he does not run the risk, as an accused does, of conviction for a new offense because of the prejudice instilled in the jury by the knowledge that he has been branded a criminal before. Although the law does not wantonly destroy people's reputations, it allows no man a better reputation than that to which he is entitled and any true assessment of a man's entitlement must include his previous convictions.

Some courts try to limit such evidence to convictions for crimes of "moral turpitude" for the purposes of attacking a witness's character, but this limitation is fraught with difficulty and is rapidly being abandoned in this and other contexts. The fact is that a conviction for almost any offense proved against a witness in court will tend to diminish his reputation rather than enhance it.

A witness may wonder where the opposition counsel ever gets to know the secrets of his past. The answer is, in major pieces of litigation, he will ferret them out as an ordinary piece of trial strategy. Investigators are commonly employed by both sides to look into the backgrounds of those who will be called as witnesses by their opponents. These investigators are often ex-police officers with experience in tracing the activities of witnesses and finding the "inside story" if any. Through various sources, including the contacts that they maintain with the police force, they can ascertain whether a prospective witness has a criminal record and other matters that probably the witness will not volunteer if he can avoid it. There is a discernable trend to legal restriction of private snooping of this nature, but it is only just beginning and for the moment private detectives are free to make inquiries as they see fit. Where this type of investigation becomes intensive, there is some question whether the morale of our society should be chilled by the caution which is induced by knowing one is being watched, all for the sake of a private legal battle.

A second way in which a witness may suffer a blow to his reputation is by the deplorable practice of allowing a psychiatrist or psychologist to testify as an expert as to the mental condition of a witness. The expert is, of course, adduced by the other side with the deliberate intention of casting doubt on the witness's reliability; unless the expert was willing to say things to the witness's detriment the opposition would not call him. This is a scandalous and most unfair use of the power to call opinion evidence, contrary to the rule that excludes matter which is more prejudicial than probative. This type of expertise is dubious to begin with, since the expert gives his opinion, not on the basis of a clinical examination of the witness (which the witness could and would refuse to submit to) but on the basis of observation of the witness in court! As we know from previous chapters, observations are notoriously unreliable, as are assessments based on demeanor, and although a psychologist may be a more skilled observer than the average, it is not regarded as good professional procedure to diagnose a person without testing, interview and observation in controlled surroundings.

Nevertheless, many courts allow this sort of impeachment, which was first ruled admissible in the federal courts in 1950 in the famous case of Alger Hiss. In that case, Mr. Hiss was accused by one Whittaker Chambers of being a Communist agent. Mr. Hiss was a senior civil servant and naturally took the accusation amiss. In two notable trials, Mr. Chambers repeated his allegations and was on the witness stand for many hours enduring cross-examination. It is generally agreed by those who made a study of the proceedings that Mr. Chambers managed to acquit himself well under cross-examination, having regard to the sensational nature of his accusations and the pressure which he was under. In view of this, Mr. Hiss's lawyers sought to discredit Chambers through psychiatric testimony of Dr. Carl Binger. Dr. Binger had not examined Mr. Chambers, and indeed his sole knowledge of him was gained through seeing him on the stand in court. Nevertheless, he gave the court his opinion that:

> "Mr. Chambers is suffering from a condition known as psychopathic personality, a disorder of character the distinguishing features of which are a-moral and asocial behavior [including] chronic, persistent, and repetitive lying; acts of deception and misrepresentation; alcoholism and drug addiction; abnormal sexuality; vagabondage, panhandling, inability to form stable attachments, and a tendency to make false accusations."

It does not require great perspicacity to see that this was a grave attack on Chambers's character in the guise of an expert opinion and a lay witness who tried to deliver this sort of innuendo would be promptly stopped. It amounts to mud-slinging of a most vicious type, completely unsupported by a factual basis. What the doctor was saying in effect was: "I am good at assessing people by watching them: I do not need to have them as patients to sum them up psychologically and neither do I need other data." One might think poorly of a doctor who professed the physical side of medicine who claimed to be able to discern cancer on the same flimsy observation.

There is another fundamental evidentiary objection to admission of this kind of testimony; it usurps the function of the jury in assessing credibility. It has long been a principle of evidentiary law that no witness must be asked to give his opinion on the very question that the court is convened to decide. Naturally, one of the questions every court has to decide is the credibility of the witnesses who parade before it. Yet here, Dr. Binger in effect says that Chambers is a liar. The difficulty is that an opinion (especially one based on the total lack of evidence that supported Dr. Binger's opinion) cannot be disproved, but only discredited. Thus, the opposition is at a great disadvantage in dealing with experts who are allowed to express their opinions. Yet, in spite of the manifest objections to this sort of testimony, it has been permitted in several states and in the system of military justice.

The philosophical basis of impeachment by allegations of previous untruthfulness or a psychological tendency to mendacity is by no means as justifiable as many people think. Suppose that it can be proved that a witness has lied in the past and has a twisted psychology that leads him to lie: it does not show logically or actually that he is still lying, or that any tendency to lie is foremost in what he now says. What is important is whether a witness is lying now, not whether he has lied in the past, and the relationship between past and present conduct is a tricky one, because the incentives to lie are variable. For an actual example, we may take the prosecution witness who admits to a defense attorney on cross-examination:

"I always lie to the F.B.I. "

"You <u>always</u> lie to the F.B.I. ?"

"Oh, yes--I have a lot to hide. "

"You have a lot to hide?"

"I had a lot to hide from the F.B.I. "

The witness here is making a perfectly reasonable point. He does not deny that he has lied to the F.B.I. because it was in his interests to do so; but he nevertheless maintains that what he is now telling the court is true. Indeed, there must be few people in the world who have not at some time or other told a lie; but that does not show them to be generally unreliable people. Attacks on the credibility of witnesses are often made as a substitute for attacks on the substance of what they said, for the simple reason that substantially their testimony cannot be refuted. An attack on credibility is essentially a diversionary tactic designed to emphasize the weakness of the source of information beyond its content.

The proof of prior inconsistent statements by a witness proceeds along the same basic lines. Here, the contention is not so much that the witness is deliberately untruthful but that he is unreliable in his observation and memory. As we have seen from our earlier chapters, this allegation can be made against most of us to some extent because of the nature of human powers. But the most damaging practical evidence of this fallibility of a witness is to produce a prior inconsistent statement made by him. This is the commonest means of impeaching a witness, and can be used to deadly effect. Its effectiveness is enhanced by the rule that although prior inconsistent statements may not be put to a witness on cross examination, prior consistent statements may not be put to him by the party calling him. This means that a witness shown to have made some inconsistent statement in the past cannot be rehabilitated in the jury's eyes by showing that the overwhelming amount of his testimony is quite consistent with what he has said on the stand. The result is that the jury have no way of knowing the total picture; they just have the blemishes on the witness's record brought to their attention.

68

A prior statement of a witness cannot be introduced into evidence as proof of the facts which it alleges, but only for purposes of impeachment, so that where a conflict between past statement and present testimony is shown it is not permissible for opposition counsel to argue that either version is proved or disproved thereby. Rather, his argument will be case in terms of the doubt it throws upon the testimony before the court. He may not properly argue that the existence of a prior inconsistent statement "proves" that the present testimony is wrong, because it can quite possibly be the present testimony that is right and the prior statement that is incorrect. Neither may he argue that the past statement is the true one, because the past statement is not before the court as evidence of its truth, but only as evidence of the witness's inconsistency. Furthermore, it is possible that neither pronouncement of the witness is correct, and that truth lies in some other direction entirely.

A witness may draw two practical lessons from these warnings regarding comparisons of statements. The first is that much careful consideration should be given to whether a witness wishes to make any statements before trial; after all, he is under no obligation to do so. If he does, the strong likelihood is that they will fall into the hands of opposition counsel because of rules which force mutual disclosure of evidence on parties to a civil dispute prior to trial, and partial disclosure by prosecution to defense in a criminal proceeding. There are circumstances where a witness has no choice but to testify--for instance, if he is summoned before a grand jury--but in most instances, he can elect to keep silent.

The second lesson is that a witness who has made statements relating to a case prior to trial should obtain copies before he is called to the stand and study them closely. In this way, he can minimize the risk of being caught unawares by a previous statement of his own that he is forgotten. Of course, his obligation on the stand is to recount his present recollection and if it disagrees with a previous statement, he must admit it. But there is every good reason to refresh his present recollection from looking at his earlier statements.

This advice applies not only to formal statements given to officials but to any given informally to newspaper reporters or even casually to inquirers. There is a common misconception that this kind of material is not admissible in court. Actually, it is not admissible as evidence of its truth because it is hearsay, of which the recounters have no personal knowledge. But it is admissible for purpose of contradicting the person who is alleged to have made the statement, just as formal statements are.

A less common means of impeachment relates to bias. Bias may be defined as a tendency to favor one side to litigation regardless of the merits of his claim. Bias may exist without any discernible interest to support it. Interest is provable because it is assumed to influence a person's judgment; few people are prepared to speak ill of someone from whom they receive benefits which would be like killing the goose that lays a golden egg. But bias can be shown without any motive to support it as bearing upon a witness's credibility. It is rare that bias can be shown explicitly, but it does happen if the witness has given vent to his prejudices before trial. This is another factor that may be revealed from careful pre-trial research. It follows that a witness who has kept to himself over the years is the one least open to attack and an opinionated person whose views have been extensively recorded (as, for example, a public figure) may be confronted with his past. It is in recognition of this vulnerability that lawyers have an addage: "Would that mine enemy had written a book", for a book will almost certainly provide some clue as to how the author's mind works and illuminate his likes and dislikes, sympathies and anathemas.

There is, however, one major difference between impeachment for an inconsistent statement and attempted impeachment for bias, proved by past statements. Bias, by its nature, is a matter of attitude, not fact and it is perfectly honorable for a person to change his bias, or point of view. Indeed, anyone whose opinions never changed at all might be suspected of inflexibility and dogmatism or, in some areas of human endeavor, plain stupidity. A scientist who would not change his opinions about a variety of matters studied in the last thirty years would not command much respect for intellect or common sense.

The distinction between facts and one's attitude to those facts is often a fine one, and some would say a non-existent one. In everyday conversation, we very rarely make an effort to be objective. Many of our statements of "fact" in everyday talk have a strong built-in bias in them, which is not always apparent to our listeners or ourselves. For example, if we have had the misfortune to be in a traffic accident, we may explain it to our friends by saying "This idiot crashed into me." In truth, this statement masquerades as fact, but is highly partial. It records the fact that a collision occurred, but slants the report by suggesting that he crashed into us, rather than we crashed into him. Furthermore, we probably have no objective evidence that he is an idiot; we have no measure of his intelligence or mentality generally, and are basing our poor view of his capacities almost solely upon our view that he was in the wrong in getting involved in a collision with us. Third, it personalizes the event of the accident to a high degree; what truly happened was that two automobiles collided, which was under the control of human beings; the form of the report which we give to our friends is in the personal form that accuses a person (with human, not automotive, characteristics of idiocy) of crashing into "us". Lastly, the statement, question-begging as it is, may well conceal more of the truth than it reveals, since it gives no data upon which our friends may judge who, if anyone, was truly to blame for the collision.

Many people find it difficult to accept that most of our thinking is as partial and sloppy as that. "There may be some people who think like that, but not me, " is a perfectly human reaction to a challenge to our intellectual abilities and our fairness. Alas, there are very few people who do not mold the facts to fit a pattern which they will find congenial in retrospect. A count of the people who will admit to having faults would reveal that there are fewer of them than those who admit to having virtues. And it is a fairly constant part of the human condition that most people believe faults to exist in larger measure in other people than they do in themselves. The human being is a rag-bag of prejudice, delusions, illusions and misapprehensions and his claim to be a rational animal is overstated. A human being selects his facts to prove the points he wants to make and eliminates from his calculations facts that do not fit; he is contradictory in his conclusions and irrational in his motives. He fits the facts to his conclusions rather than the conclusions to his facts; there are instances in history which chronicle such mistakes. He reduces events to a pattern, even though perhaps no pattern truly exists; but it is a convenient way for him to classify and package things in his memory.

Unconscious bias and "slanting" of the facts inevitably arises when parties to litigation take the stand and, as lawyers say, much "hard swearing" goes on. The distortion of the facts that takes place when a party testifies is often a subtle one, because the party really believes his own account of what happened--otherwise, he would probably not have litigated at all.

Throughout the history of the law, until the nineteenth century, parties to litigation were incompetent as witnesses on their own behalf, partly in order to avoid the clear conflict of their interest in the outcome of litigation and their duty as witnesses to tell the truth. Judge Medina, of the Second Circuit Court of Appeals remarked, in <u>United States</u> v. <u>Scully</u> 225 F2d 113 (1955): "As many of us learned for the first time when reading Dickens's 'Pickwick Papers', parties, including a defendant in a criminal case, were not competent to testify at common law, although in treason cases, and perhaps others, a defendant was sometimes permitted to make an unsworn statement." However, the right to make an unsworn statement was never accorded to parties in civil cases. Today, parties are always permitted to testify, but never required to. If they do, then of course their interest in the litigation is taken into account in assessing credibility. The reason the law was changed was that in many instances, the disqualification of an interested witness meant that the person who knew most about the facts in issue was unable to reveal it.

The final observation about these methods of impeachment is that their weight is for the jury to decide. There is a regrettable laxity in many courts in letting lawyers express their own opinions about the credibility of witnesses when they sum up to the jury. In the Hiss trial, defense counsel told the jury of the chief prosecution witness: "I would not believe him if the F.B.I. erected a stack of Bibles as high as the building," a most improper remark because the lawyer's opinion is quite irrelevant and because as it happens this form of words amounts to an imputation of perjury which would be inadmissible even if made by a duly sworn witness. Nevertheless, it was allowed to pass without reprimand by the judge.

We may conclude by pointing out that the rules relating to impeachment of witnesses can be used as instruments of muckraking. The much-vaunted "right to privacy" does not protect a witness, validly subpoenaed, from having his unsavory past publicized in court. But a witness will not find it attractive to avoid the possibility that his reputation will be damaged by refusing to testify. This sort of refusal is punishable as contempt of court in all jurisdictions, either by fine or imprisonment, or both. The only way that this sort of contempt can be "purged" is by agreeing to testify. The Organized Crime Control Act of 1970 designates witnesses who refuse "without just cause shown to comply with an order of the court to testify or provide other information . . ." (section 301) as "recalcitrant witnesses". It may be said with confidence that a fear on the part of a witness that his reputation will be damaged if he appears will not amount to "just cause shown" within the meaning of the Act.

Occasionally, for good cause, a court will permit a witness to testify without giving his name, or direct that press and other media not print the name if it is announced in court. There must be special reasons for giving a witness this privilege, however, which amount to more than mere shyness, or the desire to avoid a scandal, or the fear of damage to reputation. The court is most disposed to grant an application for anonymity if a witness is a juvenile, or has acted as an informer for the police, or has relations who will suffer unnecessarily if his name is publicly disclosed. A witness can never avoid some clues to his identity being disclosed, because for one thing he must appear in court personally. He will not be allowed to appear in a mask, so that his face cannot be seen, and it will be contempt of court for him to disguise himself. The reason for this is that the court expects to be able to judge a witness's demeanor on the stand, which is impossible if judge, lawyers and jurors cannot see him. The right to be confronted by one's accusers means complete confrontation. Just as a party to litigation cannot lawfully conceal his true identity, neither can a witness. An attempt to testify anonymously may also be a violation of the constitutional right to a public trial that is guaranteed to every criminal accused.

A witness who wishes to keep out of the limelight should raise the possibility in advance of trial, for it may require a special motion to be made to the court. The chances of gaining permission to testify anonymously are extremely small, but occasionally it is granted. However, a self-conscious or embarrassed witness may have some success in appealing to the reporters who cover the case; they may be sympathetic and avoid mentioning a witness's name. This, of course, is a purely informal way of arranging anonymity, and depends on the whims of the reporters concerned.

Chapter X

PRIVILEGE

Giving evidence in court is not like telling a story outside the courtroom for it has always been recognized that in the interests of justice there are some matters which may be spoken of with more freedom in court than outside and, conversely, there are certain matters which may be referred to with less freedom than in ordinary conversation. All of the major rules which illustrate this principle are called "privileges" in law, but in fact they are widely different. It is to the advantage of anyone who expects to give testimony to be acquainted with these rules.

The Law of Defamation

Defamation is a tort, or civil wrong, which can take two forms: libel, which is written or otherwise in permanent form, and slander, which is committed by making imputations by spoken word. In everyday conversation, unflattering comments about someone else may be actionable as slander if they fall into certain categories and are denied by the plaintiff. A libel is actionable if it imputes anything to the plaintiff which is calculated to lower him in the eyes of his fellow citizens, again provided they are denied by him. The relevance of this law to court proceedings is obvious; many of the things said in judicial proceedings are uncomplimentary and disputed by the people to whom they relate. A person accused of murder who pleads not guilty will be anxious to dispute the testimony of the prosecution that tends to show him guilty. Since an accusation of murder is a most serious one, it could well be the ground of a suit for defamation if made outside court. But the proceedings in court are privileged and as such they protect all witnesses from suits for libel and slander based on what they say in court. The purpose of this privilege is naturally to encourage the utmost candor in witnesses, so that the court may get at the truth.

However, this privilege is misunderstood by many people and a witness should be warned that it has its limitations. Although allegations made in court are privileged, those made outside remain governed by the normal law. A witness who repeats an allegation outside the courtroom may be held liable for defamation for that statement, because the privilege no longer attaches to him. Suppose that during the course of a trial a witness makes an imputation of drug addiction against Smith. The witness is protected whether or not he is right in believing Smith is a drug addict, because what he says in court is privileged. But if, after the proceedings are over, the witness persists in spreading the rumor that Smith is an addict, Smith may sue for defamation and the witness will find himself defending an expensive suit, in which it will be his burden to show on a preponderance of the evidence that Smith is an addict. It will be no defense to the action that he was merely repeating the allegation made in previous legal proceedings unless the court found as a fact that Smith was an addict, and even then the issue may be re-tried in some circumstances. A witness should not let the freedom and privilege he enjoys in court loosen his tongue on subsequent, unprivileged, occasions.

Privilege against Self-Incrimination

The major type of privilege apart from that relating to confidential communications is famous as the privilege against self-incrimination. Unlike the privilege of confidentiality, this privilege has its foundations in the Constitution, Amendment V of which provides that "no person . . . shall be compelled, in any criminal case, to be witness against himself . . . ." When this Amendment was passed in 1791, no one foresaw what a legal tangle these few words would cause to succeeding generations.

A first point about this provision of the Fifth Amendment should be that, like the privilege of confidences explained in the ensuing section of this chapter, it must be expressly claimed. This at once causes some difficulties: it means that a witness must impliedly admit that he is open to incrimination and hence his reputation tends to suffer anyway. Although judges customarily charge juries that they ought not to draw any inference from a witness's refusal to answer questions on the ground that he might incriminate himself and that it is "as if the questions had never been asked," common sense tells the jury that it is not so. It is a most grievous blow to some witnesses' reputations, but they must claim the privilege if they are to have its benefit. There is another problem, too: that to be able to claim the privilege, a witness must know what is criminal and what is not, in spite of the fact that this is not always an easy conclusion to reach. Although ignorance of the law is no excuse, it is widespread and one cannot help feeling pity for someone who fails to claim privilege on the ground that it might incriminate him because he does not think he has committed a crime and subsequently finds out he is mistaken. Luckily, this happens rarely, but the possibility remains, for it was decided in United States v. Scully 225 F2d 113 (2d Cir. 1955) that there is no need to warn a witness of his danger of self-incrimination, at least when he is testifying before a grand jury. This was held in spite of the realization a prosecutor might know full well that a witness was, metaphorically speaking, about to slip his head into the noose. As Circuit Judge Frank said:

> "It is not too difficult to justify that ruling when the prosecutor has no good reason to believe that an answer to a question will tend to incriminate. However, when, as in the instant case, a question is such that the prosecutor cannot help knowing that the answer will incriminate the witness, much can be said in favor of a warning requirement. Particularly is that so when the witness is before a grand jury, for then he cannot have his counsel present to call his attention to his privilege."

Nevertheless, Judge Frank went on to agree with the holding of the Second Circuit Court of Appeals on the ground that it seemed consonant with Supreme Court decisions in that area.

The Confidential Privilege

There are very few things that are considered confidential in a court of law. The most intimate revelations may be made in court and little heed is paid to the embarrassment of witnesses who must make them. The mere fact that one person says something to another that is "secret" will not bring the privilege for confidential communications into operation. Still less will a clandestine action be considered confidential, or else most criminals would be outside the ambit of the law, since they commit crimes with the intention that they remain secret. Rather, the law has narrowly circumscribed the privilege so that it extends to a few relationships, such as those of doctor and patient, priest and penitent, lawyer and client, husband and wife. Things said between these people may not generally be compulsorily disclosed in a courtroom. However, the privilege may always be waived by the non-professional party to these communications; in other words, a patient can always give his doctor permission to reveal what was said while they were consulting, a penitent can allow a priest to reveal his confession and a client can let his lawyer tell what passed between them. On the other hand, a doctor, priest, or lawyer may not do so without permission. To give just cause for withholding testimony the privilege must be specifically claimed --that is what the Organized Crime Control Act means when it says that cause must be shown. Although this Act applies only in federal courts, the principle applies in all state courts, too, and a failure to claim privilege expressly will rebound to the detriment of a witness.

In view of this and other rulings, a witness who believes he may wish to claim privilege in court should always take legal advice in advance. This possibility that confidential data may be touched upon in the course of examination can usually be foreseen, and a witness knows perfectly well whether there are skeletons in his closet which might be a basis for raising the self-incrimination privilege. In both instances, the interest of the witness may be vitally at stake and be at variance with the party who has called him. It is therefore unwise to rely simply on the advice of the party's counsel, since he is not disinterested and his first duty is to his client.

Chapter XI

THE AVAILABILITY OF EVIDENCE

Tradition has it that Mrs. Beeton, the authoress of a distinguished nineteenth century cookbook, began her recipe for cooking goose with the practical advice: "First catch your goose." Intending litigants might similarly be exhorted: "First catch your witness," for a surprisingly large number of lawsuits are commenced by people who turn out to be unable to sustain the burden of proof they must carry in order to win. The law imposes almost no restriction upon the right to start litigation, no matter how ill-advised it may appear. The reasons for this are two: that freedom of access to the courts must be maintained if any semblance of fairness is to remain in the law, and that the courts cannot fruitfully prejudge a case; if they are to spend time considering whether an action should be allowed to be brought they might just as well proceed to the merits of the case and use the time to settle the issues between the parties once and for all. The consequence of this lack of restriction on litigation is that a proportion of the actions commenced each year have no reasonable chance of success because the plaintiff's complaint against the defendant cannot be backed by competent evidence from witnesses who can testify to material facts. Most plaintiffs believe that victory will be theirs, but not all of them have good grounds for their belief; lawsuits are built upon their initiators' sense of grievance rather than a careful and objective consideration of the adequacy of evidence available. Lawyers are wary of clients who have good cases which they are unable to prove, but it often happens that the weakness of the evidence is not immediately obvious to a lawyer when he is first consulted, and hence suits are started notwithstanding a paucity of proof. Even in circumstances where it is beyond doubt that witnesses exist, they can be very elusive; the availability of witnesses is a variable which has great influence over the whole legal system.

It was pointed out in Chapter I that the power to compel a witness to appear by issuing a subpoena was basic to the working of our system of criminal justice, because it allowed even an unpopular litigant to obtain testimony favorable to his cause. The subpoena power is useless, however, if a litigant does not know on whom he may fruitfully serve a subpoena; he must be able to identify those people with information helpful to his case. This can be a severe difficulty if a litigant has been involved in a widely observed incident, but the crowd that observed it has dispersed. The litigant would probably wish to interview all members of the crowd to ascertain what they had seen, if only he knew who and where they were! His chances of finding every member of the crowd are poor; but if he has enough energy, time and money at his disposal he can be sure of reaching more members than if he merely waited for them to contact him. In situations like this, careful pre-trial investigation can produce many helpful pieces of evidence; a shrewd investigator can "mine" for witnesses just as a prospector mines for gold. Once the investigator has sifted his evidence, he can see the real strength or weakness of his case as it will appear in court.

The ability of a litigant to reach witnesses in this way in practice depends on how much money he has to spend. Investigation costs a lot and can be a substantial burden on a litigant of modest means. In this respect, the law reflects not so much equality before the law, as the fact that a litigant gets what he pays for. Some jurisdictions pay the investigation expenses of a criminal defendant in certain circumstances; but none pay them in purely private civil suits, where a rich litigant is at a substantial advantage. The dividends that intensive pre-trial investigation can bring are in no way related to the practice of bribery, discussed on page 51. The witnesses that may be found as a result of investigation are not brought forward because of a corrupt payment, but simply because they will not come forward of their own accord; they are waiting for the initiative to come from someone else. As soon as they have been contacted by a litigant or his representative they are happy to talk.

The need to ferret out witnesses arises out of the process of self-selection which witnesses themselves engage in. Some people come forward to volunteer their services; some deliberately avoid witness duty because it is onerous and ill-paid; most are indifferent and apathetic and will do nothing unless and until they are asked to. It is a constant source of amazement to lawyers and laymen alike that potential witnesses with vital information at their disposal are uncovered by investigations, who can and do make a material difference to the outcome of a trial. In searching out evidence, as in other things, persistence pays. One reason for this is that litigation rarely appears as important to a potential witness as to a litigant himself; the witness is probably indifferent to the outcome of the proceedings which do not affect his interests, or affect them only very remotely. The chances are, in most instances, that a potential witness does not even know that litigation has commenced regarding the matter on which he has knowledge. Even if he did, he cannot reasonably be expected to find out the details of the suit, such as where the action has been commenced, in which court and who the parties are.

One particularly important factor which affects the availability of testimony is that witnesses die between the events giving rise to suit and the time of trial. The law's delays are proverbial; in many jurisdictions it is common that it takes several years from the commencement of a suit to bring it on to trial. In the nature of things, it is inevitable that a substantial number of prospective witnesses will die in the intervening years, with the consequence that one side or the other has its case severely weakened. In some instances, courts will accept transcribed statements of those who have died but on the whole the probative weight of such written evidence is less than if the decedent had appeared in court, for the same reasons as were discussed in relation to depositions by living witnesses in Chapter VI. However, where a written statement was made by a witness who is dead at the time of the legal proceedings into which it has been introduced it may often be taken as evidence of the truth of what it says, whereas a written statement made by a witness still living can normally only be used to demonstrate inconsistency in the witness's recollection.

Another aspect of the problem created by the death of prospective witnesses is highlighted by the so-called "dead man statutes," mentioned earlier on page 48. These statutes prevent testimony being given as to the intentions or acts of a decedent by one who seeks to share in the decedent's estate, if the purpose of the testimony is to establish the claim to a share of the estate, or enlarge the share. These statutes have been widely criticized because they may defeat a perfectly just claim, but they remain the law in a number of states. The idea behind this sort of legislation is that a claimant might tell a completely untrue story in order to establish a right to a deceased's property knowing full well that no one could contradict him because the deceased himself left no record to contradict the claimant's allegations. This difficulty arises because the law recognizes oral dispositions of personal property in certain circumstances. Thus, if a claimant alleges that a dead man indicated a wish that his personal property should be transferred to the claimant, it may be viewed as a valid gift, or other disposition. The dead man statutes defeat such claims by an evidentiary rule. As a further complication to the law, in some states the defendant executors of a deceased person may waive their right to plead the dead man statute. Some executors have done so with the consequence that the plaintiff has succeeded in his claim against the estate - see, for an example Oliver v. Campbell 43 Cal. 2d 298, 273 PP. 2d 15 (1954) Results such as this should stand as a warning to executors of the dangers of waiving rights under the "dead man" legislation. The effects of the "dead man" legislation may be summarized as follows, where a plaintiff claims that by virtue of action and words of a person now dead, a valid claim against his estate may be made:

1. The dead man statute may prevent evidence being admitted for the purpose of establishing the claim;

2. The dead man statute may be waived by the executor, with the result that the claimant wins or loses on the merits.

3. It may be held that the dead man statute is inapplicable, and therefore the case is heard on the merits.

The modern trend is to repeal "dead man statute" and replace it with provisions permitting testimony relating to the claim against a decedent's estate providing that some material portion of it is corroborated. This was the recommendation of the Law Revision Commission of the state of Michigan in its First Annual Report in 1966. According to that report "the requirement of corroboration coupled with the availability of modern pleading and discovery procedures will materially reduce the possibility of false testimony." However, that optimistic view must be weighed against the commission's insistence that "it is not intended that every portion of the survivor's testimony need be corroborated." The fact is that a clever liar will almost certainly be able to weave a plausible tale which is corroborated in a material respect, because the particular evidence which is corroborated is true; the remaining part of the tale (which the Commission's reform does not require to be corroborated) will be the false part. It seems dubious that the supposed safeguard of corroboration is really an effective one, and it might be better simply to repeal the dead man statute and substitute no alternative legislation. The risk of perjury, after all, is one that the courts face in all litigations, not merely those involving claims against a dead man's estate and one cannot consistently argue for corroboration of only one element of a story as a worthwhile protection.

The other major area in which witness-availability becomes of importance is created by the law relating to re-opening a case in which new evidence appears subsequent to trial. This happens on a surprising number of occasions. In criminal trials, there is always the possibility of achieving a pardon for a person whom new evidence reveals to have been wrongly convicted. An unsatisfactory aspect of this is that pardons are given on a discretionary basis, by members of the executive rather than judicial officers. It is much to be desired that all criminal jurisdictions enact provisions which allow appellate courts to reverse and remand for new trial cases where a convict can produce new evidence which tends to throw doubt upon the correctness of his conviction. Unfortunately, few states have such legislation, and those that do have hedged around the provisions in such a way that they do not serve justice in all the circumstances they might. One suspects that a certain amount of legal amour propre is involved here; the courts are not keen to operate a statute which may expose their fallibility. The commonest restriction upon re-opening a criminal case where the defendant proffers new evidence is that he must show that it was not available at the time of the trial, and could not have been acquired by the defendant at the time by due diligence, and in point of fact was not so acquired. The trouble with this sort of formulation is that the courts impose high standards of due diligence upon criminal defendants who had little financial backing when they were preparing their defense. In this respect, once more, the limitations of a small budget put a defendant at a disadvantage. He may not have been in a position to seek out the evidence which has now come into his hands; it would have been too expensive to do so. This sort of problem frequently arises with the preparation of expert evidence, or chemical analyses which might have aided the defense.

In civil cases, the chances of re-opening a case because new evidence has appeared are even slimmer. It is felt - correctly in most instances - that a civil litigant should be left to his own devices in finding evidence, and he cannot expect to re-open a case which he has lost. However, there are sometimes occasions on which a new suit may be brought because the appearance of new evidence alters the issue on which the original action was based. There are a surprising number of defendants in civil suits who never enter an appearance, and who allow judgment to be entered against them without ever presenting a defense at all. A person who has never entered an appearance in a civil suit may not re-open his case in any circumstances unless he shows just cause for non-appearance on the grounds of absence of proper notice.

Chapter XII

TESTIFYING IN SPECIAL CIRCUMSTANCES

So far, this book has dealt with testimony proffered in court under normal rules of evidence and procedure, but as was pointed out in Chapter I there are circumstances in which a court may hear evidence without being bound by the normal rules and there are bodies which are not courts at all, but nevertheless hear testimony. This chapter discusses these special circumstances and the effect they have upon the presentation of a case or other matters.

The device of using testimony given by witnesses was originally adopted by courts, but a large number of other bodies have since come to appreciate its utility. The selection of examples of bodies which use testimonial evidence in this book is necessarily limited but it is hoped that it will provide some guidance to a prospective witness who has been summoned to appear before a body other than a court. Nowadays, statute has given power to many institutions to compel testimony, or has allowed such bodies to use the subpoena power of the courts in certain circumstances. The result is that many of the subpoenas which are issued do not require attendance at court, but before legislative committees, Government officials, arbitrators and commissions of inquiry.

The expansion of the subpoena power to cover the needs of many tribunals has not been one that has proceeded in a consistent or orderly fashion. Statutes granting the subpoena power have been passed as and when it was felt that a need arose in a particular sphere, and provisions have consequently not been uniform. The recipient of a subpoena to attend upon a body other than a court should check the specific power under which the summons is issued if he is in doubt as to its validity. Nevertheless it will be seen from the discussions below that all the bodies which have been given subpoenaing rights have a considerable amount of power, frequently expressed to be equal to the courts in the enabling statute.

The most important bodies to possess the power of subpoena besides courts are legislatures. It is rare that a person is summoned to testify before the whole legislature (though it is not unknown and the power exists). More typically, committees of the legislature require a witness's presence and after hearing him, report to the chamber of the legislature which appointed them.

From time to time, legislative hearings have become matters of popular interest, attaining or even surpassing the attention given to sensational criminal trials - but most testimony before legislative committees is given little publicity. Nevertheless, a witness will do well to take legal advice in advance, for though the number of people summoned before legislative committees each year is fewer than the number who testify before the courts, legislative committees have become such an important part of our governmental machinery that they deserve special attention, particularly because an appearance before one may have the most deleterious consequences for a witness's reputation.

A starting point to any discussion of legislative hearings must be that they are an American invention with no true common law precedent. Although there are superficial similarities between court procedures and committee hearings, the origins of the two are quite different. This has had the important result that Congress (and other legislatures set up by the various states) have had few historic guidelines to go by in regulating their committees, and since there is a concentration of power in the legislatures which it is not easy to challenge successfully, they have usually been generous in awarding themselves authority to investigate in the manner they please. Courts have little ability to control legislatures in this respect, unless a constitutional issue has been raised, and even this may not bring the proceedings effectively under the supervision of the courts unless the nature of the complaint overturns the presumption that a legislature intends to legislate constitutionally. The courts, in an effort to minimize the number of direct clashes with the legislatures, have recognized that generally the powers of a legislative committee have - prima facie - been whatever the legislature that set it up has said they are. A witness who has been called before such a committee has been at a consequent disadvantage in disputing the legitimacy of committee hearings because he has lacked legal authorities in his favor; not enough litigation has taken place regarding the rights and duties of legislative committees. This problem is clearly demonstrated by the controversial decisions of the Supreme Court arising out of its consideration of the doings of a subcommittee of the famous Committee on Un-American Activities of the House of Representatives, which are discussed later in this chapter. For the moment it is enough to observe that the sequence of events has always been an assertion of power by Congress, resisted by a witness and then litigated when Congress has claimed the power to punish the recalcitrant witness. It takes considerable courage for a witness to stand firm against the will of a legislature, especially when the rights and wrongs of legislative action in this field are ill-defined by the courts.

There are two great differences between appearing before a legislative committee and appearing before a court: the issues of interest to a legislature are much wider than those considered in court, and the rules of evidence do not apply to legislative hearings. It can be seen that these differences make objections of relevance and materiality somewhat difficult to sustain: just how difficult may be seen from a consideration of the statute under which Congress punishes contempt (2 U.S.C. section 192), which makes it an offense to refuse "to answer any question pertinent to the question under inquiry." How is a witness to know (a) precisely what the question under inquiry is, and (b) whether the question he is being asked is "pertinent" to the question under inquiry? On these issues, a considerable amount of litigation has been spawned. In Watkins v. United States 354 U.S. 178 (1957), Chief Justice Warren held that "it is the duty of the investigative body, upon objection of the witness on grounds of pertinency, to state for the record the subject under inquiry at that time and the manner in which the propounded questions are pertinent thereto." This formulation, though helpful to some degree, will not solve the dilemma of a witness who is dissatisfied with the committee's explanation; if he believes it is inadequate and the committee refuses to expand on its explanation he will be forced to answer, or risk prosecution for contempt.

The determination of whether a question put by a legislative committee must be answered or not is made especially hard by the fact that all members of a committee may speak for it. Most trial courts have only one judge and what he says is reliable as the court's view, but that sort of certainty is not available to a witness before a legislative hearing. One legislator after another may chip in with his view of a question and it is rare that the committee's chairman makes any formal ruling in the way that a judge does. The result is that on appeal to the courts, the whole record is reviewed to see whether overall the pertinency of the questions asked has been demonstrated. It is noteworthy that members of legislative committees are frequently partisan in backing up their colleagues in asking a question to which a witness has taken objection, and act as prosecutor, judge and jury combined. The net result can be to "pillory"a witness, and as the dissenting minority put it in Barenblatt v. United States 360 U.S. 109 (1959), to punish a witness "by humiliation and public shame."

The interests of the legislators who are members of committees are quite opposed to those of the witnesses who may be summoned before them. A witness may wish to keep some aspects of his activities or beliefs private, whereas a senator or representative may be keen to gain kudos by "exposing" him. The more sensational the exposure, the more likely it is that a legislator will receive publicity as a crusader for the public good. Even elected public prosecutors do not have the freedom that a member of a congressional committee has to ask all sorts of wide-ranging questions of a witness, because the rules of evidence prevent them. Furthermore, there are procedural bars to hounding a witness in the way it is possible to do in a legislative committee. A witness in committee may suffer cross-examination from several legislators although a criminal defendant only faces one cross-examiner.

In theory, all investigative hearings held by legislatures must have a legislative purpose - that is, must have the potential to inform and aid the legislature in passing new legislation or repealing the old. This limitation does not have much practical effect on the conduct of hearings because almost any subject may be appropriate for legislative action and it is hard to show that a hearing, or part of it, is devoid of legislative purpose. It has, on occasion, been achieved: see United States v. Icardi 140 F.

Supp. 383 (D.C.D.C., 1956), in which a subcommittee of the Armed Services Committee of Congress was held to have acted in an unauthorized manner in probing the guilt of a witness brought before it of certain crimes.

It is open to doubt whether the procedure of calling witnesses before a legislative committee is truly an effective means of "informing" a legislature with a view to passing legislation. It is true that the method brings a variety of informed parties before a section of the legislature - but whether they manage to impart their information to the committee members is a different matter. Similarly, one may question whether the testimony heard by committees of this sort is likely to represent a balance of opinion. On many issues there are more witnesses who wish to see legislation passed than do not, because the informed people who do not wish to see legislation are not so eager to come forward and because the thrust of their testimony will necessarily be negative. Hearings have a way of exaggerating the things that are wrong and focussing on small sub-issues rather than the general state of the subject under discussion.

The principle of Watkins and all the decisions that followed in its wake is easy to state in its essence: a witness has the right to know why a question is being asked before he answers it. The application of the principle is the difficulty which is not surmounted by the Supreme Court's variations on this theme, for it is possible that the witness will be dissatisfied with the reasons that the legislative committee gives. Nevertheless, unless the witness gives way and answers, or the committee agrees not to press for an answer, a prosecution for contempt under 2 U.S.C. Section 192 will follow. Judgments of "pertinency" are after all matters of degree and it is possible that a witness and a committee may in good faith disagree about where to draw the line. The weakness of the Watkins line of cases is that they do not explain where the line should be drawn.

Regulatory Agencies

This century has seen the formation of many Governmental agencies with massive powers of regulation. To them, legislative assemblies have delegated much "rule-making" power in particular spheres. Examples on a federal level are the Securities and Exchange Commission (S.E.C.); the Federal Communications Commission and the Food and Drug Administration. The department of Justice, in its various subdivisions, has considerable regulatory power, particularly in its anti-trust division and through the immigration and Naturalization Service.

Since each regulatory agency was set up under separate statutes, generalizations in this field are difficult. Nevertheless, all major federal agencies have the statutory authority to hold hearings on matters within their field of interest, and in pursuance of that power are given subpoena power. Professor Bernard Schwartz, in his Commentary on the Constitution of the United States, published in 1968, finds that the power is commonly given as a matter of course, and that award of the power no longer seems to stir the uneasiness which it did when it was a novelty.

Most hearings held by regulatory agencies affect the interests of only a limited class of persons in a limited sphere, but that does not mean that ordinary members of the public do not get involved. Sometimes, where a regulatory agency is entitled to fix rates and tariffs for various services, or grant licenses and franchises as the Federal Communications Commission does to T.V. stations, the views of the public are solicited by the agencies themselves. In such areas of public concern almost any member of the public is entitled to make his views known, though there is never a right to be heard at a hearing simply by virtue of being a member of the public. If one is specially affected by a proposal, however, there may indeed be a right to be heard.

Regulatory agencies have to deal with matters which are somewhat specialized. Unless a witness appears before them at his own request, therefore, he is unlikely to be subpoenaed before one unless he is an expert of some kind. The branch of law dealing with the regulatory agencies has come to be known as "administrative law" and occupies a large number of the legal practitioners in Washington D.C., as well as some elsewhere.

Almost certainly, a witness called before a regulatory agency will have strong views on the issue to be determined. It may be that this is the very reason for his testimony being solicited, since a regulatory hearing may receive expressions of opinion even from witnesses who are not, in the strict sense used by courts, experts. Regulation of the vast industries now under the sway of the federal Government attracts the attention of lobbyists like a magnet, and many of the witnesses who appear in regulatory hearings tend to be advocates of a particular point of view rather than witnesses of fact. This is not always so, and it is not always explicit, but there is a tendency that way.

The importance of the regulatory agencies varies considerably, but everyone is affected by their work. They control, to a greater or lesser extent, the television we watch, the railroads we use, the food we eat and the drugs we take and many other facets of our lives.

Federal Tax Investigations

The Internal Revenue Code of 1954 contains special provisions relating to the examination of witnesses by officials of the Treasury department during an investigation of a person's tax liability. Section 7602 provides:

> "For the purpose of ascertaining the correctness of any return, making a return where none has been made, determining the liability of any person for any internal revenue tax or the liability at law or in equity of any transferee or fiduciary of any person in respect of any internal revenue tax, or collecting any such liability, the Secretary or his delegate is authorized ...(2) to summon the person liable for tax or required to perform the act, or any officer or employee of such person, or any person having possession, custody, or care of books of account containing entries relating to the business of the person liable for tax or required to perform the act, or any other person the Secretary or his delegate may deem proper...."

The references to "the Secretary" in this section refer to the Secretary of the Treasury, who is given wide powers in tracking down seeming tax-evaders. The power of summons enacted by section 7602 is a much wider one than that usually encountered because it is not confined to giving testimony in court. On the contrary, the I.R.S. may designate the place to which a person is summoned for the inquiry, which need not be a court. The only restrictions upon the Secretary's power which apply generally are that the time and place of examination shall be "reasonable under the circumstances" (Section 7605 (a)), and that no taxpayer shall be subjected to unnecessary examination (Section 7605 (b)), and it will be seen that in practice these are not substantial limitations. Reasonableness of time and place may allow the inquiry to be held at a District office of the I.R.S., or other premises if the District office is far away from the person summoned, and it seems probable that an inquiry set within any normal business hours poses no problem. As for the restriction of the Secretary's power to necessary examination, it is difficult to see that this imposes any real inhibition on the Treasury's powers at all. After all, the purposes for which Section 7602 is expressed to exist make it proper for an investigation to be made to "ascertain" that the law has been complied with; one might well think that it is always necessary to investigate if it is desired to "ascertain" anything.

These important provisions of the tax law smack to some extent of "Star Chamber" procedures, in that much discretion is left in the hands of an official to probe a citizen's financial dealings outside a courtroom. It is fair to say, however, that the Internal Revenue Service enjoys a good reputation in the manner in which it uses its admittedly large powers. A witness who finds himself summoned by the I.R.S. will probably have a fair idea of the focus of the inquiry, especially if he is required not only to give testimony under oath, but to produce business or other records. Furthermore, the initiation of a formal inquiry in which the power of summons is used by the I.R.S. will probably have been preceded by correspondence with the Service, in which its field of interest will have been specified. In view of the willingness of the Service to "settle" or compromise a tax claim on terms allowing time to pay, the power of inquiry contemplated by Sections 7601 and 7602 is resorted to only where the subject taxpayer has refused to co-operate with the Treasury officials.

A person summoned to an inquiry of this nature may find himself torn between loyalty to his employer and the sanctions available to the I.R.S. if he fails to comply with the summons. Those sanctions are enforcement of the summons by a United States District Court, with the possibility of arrest and imprisonment for contempt in failing to answer. In these circumstances, most employees find that their loyalty is over-ridden by practical consideration of the possibility of punishment. Arguably, the issuance of a summons in these circumstances is a positive benefit to an employee whose employer is under suspicion of tax evasion, since by being compelled to reveal what he knows of his master's business he is effectively relieved of any choice in supporting his master or not; the threat of being held in contempt is a potent one.

Arbitrations

Arbitrations have taken over many of the traditional functions of courts in the last generation. They provide quicker, less formal disposition of business disputes than the courts and many business contracts are nowadays written with a provision for arbitration if the parties find themselves in disagreement. Arbitration differs from a court disposition of a case in several important respects:

1. An arbitrator may be chosen because of his expertise in the subject-matter of the arbitration. By contrast, a judge often has no expertise in the matter and even if he does, he may not rely upon it in reaching his decision; he must attend only to the evidence presented before him;

2. Arbitrators are not bound to give their decisions in accordance with the law; they may decide what is "fair," a freedom not permitted to a judge;

3. The rules of evidence do not apply in an arbitration, though increasingly this aspect of arbitration is changing and procedural safeguards are being built into arbitrations which have something of the same effect as rules of evidence do in courts of law.

It is an irony of recent legal history that arbitration proceedings are coming to look more and more like ordinary court cases. Arbitration achieved its popularity with the business community because it was different from the courts, including the fact that it tended to be cheaper. Nevertheless, arbitration is conducted with the aid of lawyers who have tended to import more and more of their professional standards into arbitrations. This phenomenon has been aptly described as "creeping legalism." A fundamental problem of arbitration has always been that since its effectiveness depends upon the consent of the parties, there were difficulties from the beginning in insisting that the losing party abide by an arbitrator's decision. What was to stop his appealing to the courts against the decision of the arbitrator, thereby merely using arbitration as a delaying device? The answer was "very little," until most jurisdictions passed statutes which provided, among other things, that in certain circumstances the ruling of an arbitrator has the force of a decision rendered by the ordinary courts. But within the arbitration statutes were the springs of "creeping legalism," for they enacted safeguards against arbitrary arbitrators and grossly unfair procedures. They also provided arbitrations with powers which were very similar to those possessed by courts, including the power to compel the attendance of witnesses. That power has been expressed in the various acts dealing with arbitration to be the same as, or at least similar to, the powers vested in courts.

In this connection, it is instructive to look at the powers given to arbitrators in three important pieces of legislation. A useful starting point is the Uniform Arbitration Act, Section 7 of which provides that: "the arbitrators may issue (cause to be issued) subpoenas for the attendance of witnesses...and shall have the power to administer oaths. Subpoenas so issued shall be served, and upon application to the Court by a party or the arbitrators, enforced, in the manner provided by law for the service and enforcement of subpoenas in a civil action." The same section also provides that "all provisions of law compelling a person under subpoena to testify are applicable." It will be obvious that enactments such as this make the position of an arbitrator virtually identical with that of a court in respect of compelling testimony. Yet since an arbitrator is not bound by the rules of evidence, as mentioned, one wonders how far it is proper and in the public interest to arm him with the power of subpoena - but notwithstanding any doubts about the wisdom of such a provision, it appears in other statutes besides the Uniform Act. The United States Arbitration Act (concerned largely with admiralty law) gives the power of compulsion to arbitrators by its Section 7, and Section 7505 of the New York Civil Practice Law and Rules does likewise. Section 1456 of the New York Civil Practice Act is to the same effect.

As creeping legalism has taken its hold, more and more

of the devices of the courts have been adopted by and granted to arbitration proceedings. Briefs are submitted before the hearing; witnesses may be deposed and if necessary subpoenaed; each side takes a contnetious position and may be represented by counsel; and the order of proceedings in many arbitrations is nowadays indistinguishable from that of a court. Furthermore, arbitrators are constrained by some aspects of the law. To take but one example: even though an arbitrator is entitled to decide a matter in a manner he considers just and equitable, he may not give his award to the poorer party on the ground that the other side can better afford to lose.

A witness will probably find the conditions of his testimony to be similar to those he would face in court. It is an interesting reflection on history that the arbitration acts have adopted the rule that an arbitrator may summon witnesses of his own accord, without the consent of the parties. The common law permitted a judge to summon his own witnesses, too, if he wished, but the practice has fallen into disuse. Arbitrators, however, have the power and use it. History has in this respect travelled full circle. Originally, judges and jurors were chosen for their special knowledge of the subject of litigation, on the basis that they would be most likely to give a just decision. But it is now considered quite improper for a judge or juror with first-hand knowledge of the parties or subjects involved in proceedings to sit, and judges regularly disqualify themselves from trying a case in which they have any interest of a personal or business nature. This requirement of ignorance is axiomatic as part of the modern concept of "fair trial." Yet the arbitrator today may be someone known to both the parties, and may even be involved in the same business as those who seek arbitration. He can, in fact, be chosen by the parties for the very reasons which would disqualify a judge.

One difference between appearing as a witness in court and in an arbitration is that an arbitration may be held anywhere convenient to everyone concerned and therefore may not be in a courtroom. This is reflected in the less formal atmosphere that prevails at arbitrations. Arbitrations may be held in hired rooms, or attorneys' offices or even on the business premises of one or other of the parties, though this is rare since it is preferred that the place of arbitration be neutral territory.

The procedure of arbitrators can vary, but the statutes un-

der which they operate make it clear that many of the characteristics of litigation are to be transferred to arbitration proceedings, especially in respect of treatment of witnesses. For example, Section 7506 of the New York Civil Practice Law and Rules
expressly provides that the parties have a right to cross-examine
witnesses.

Courts not Bound by Normal Rules

It may seem surprising that courts do not always follow the
rules of procedure and evidence. After all, if there are to be
rules there is much virtue in applying them consistently. Nevertheless, there are circumstances where the courts feel it proper
to dispense with the more restrictive and technical of their rules
and a prospective witness may find it useful to know of them.
There is some question whether a court may appropriately ignore
procedural rights if the proceedings are in any sense "punitive,"
because of the Constitutional guarantee of due process. Much
legal thought has been given to this problem in the last few years,
the net result of which has been to label many non-criminal proceedings as punitive which were not so considered before. The
prime examples have been in the field of juvenile and mental incompetency law.

Juveniles were dealt with in every state of the Union in a way
different from that of an adult, and usually passed through a separate system of courts. Even where the offense they were charged
with was one which would have resulted in a full-blown criminal
trial if an adult was thought to be the culprit, a juvenile would
be taken through the juvenile courts. A person was treated as a
juvenile if he was under a statutorily set age - usually sixteen
or seventeen. The philosophy behind the juvenile court system
was basically paternal; it was an attempt to shield the young from
the horrors of a criminal trial. In fact, however, the juvenile
courts were often positively disadvantageous to a young offender.
He had no rights customarily granted to an adult accused, and
in addition might find himself sent to a reform school for a longer period than he would ever have been sent to jail if he had been
convicted as an adult.

All this describes the system as it was; but in an important
Supreme Court decision in 1967, the position was fundamentally

altered to accord a juvenile the rights which he would have if he were an adult. In Re Gault 387 U.S. 1, it was held that the rights encompassed by the conception of due process should be granted to a juvenile accused. The facts of that case have a material relevance to the law relating to the appearance of a witness in a juvenile court. Gault had been found guilty of making obscene telephone calls to a neighbor. The neighbor had complained to the police and did not even appear at the juvenile court hearing, although the law would not permit an adult to be convicted of such an offense without proper proof and without giving the accused the opportunity to confront his accuser. It was held by the Supreme Court that Gault's Constitutional rights had been violated. Today, a witness who appears in a juvenile court proceeding will in all probability find that his experience is much as it would have been in an adult court. It may be wondered whether the Gault case may not sound the death toll of juvenile courts; as Professor Weinreb has observed: "Aside from the fact that a person whose case is heard and determined by the juvenile court is labeled a 'delinquent' rather than a 'criminal'" it makes little difference whether his case is tried in one court or the other. It seems clear that the present juvenile courts are not ideal and radical changes are to be expected in the next decade. Gault moves them in the direction of the adult courts' model, but that model is not one which is wholly satisfactory even for adults and adaptation of procedures to the special needs of juvenile (if, indeed, they have special needs that can be catered to) will not be an easy task. In view of the fact that an increasing number of juveniles are represented by counsel, it is likely that witnesses in the juvenile court may expect to be cross-examined in much the same way as in the adult courts.

The prognosis for committal proceedings for mental incompetents is much the same. These proceedings are capable of depriving a person of liberty by their findings, if an order is made for compulsory hospitalization. The mentally ill are entitled to the protection of procedural safeguards as much as the mentally healthy, and the trend in the courts is to accord special attention to their rights because so many of them are not capable of protecting them for themselves. It remains true that the rules of evidence do not apply with their full rigor in incompetency proceedings, but basic rights such as the right of confrontation will tend to standardize a witness's experience in the image of the ordinary courts.

Chapter XIII

IMMUNITY

Not everyone is a willing servant of justice. There are potential witnesses who do not wish to give the courts the benefit of their testimony and either refuse to appear on the stand entirely, or do so only in exchange for some important benefit. In particular, a witness who has himself been guilty of a crime may wish for assurances that he will not be prosecuted himself if he gives testimony against another which also implicates the witness. If such assurances are given, it is said that the witness has been granted "immunity" from subsequent prosecution.

A moment's consideration will show that grants of immunity are closely connected with the privilege against self-incrimination which was discussed in Chapter X. The Fifth Amendment provides that no one may be compelled to be a witness against himself. By judicial interpretation, this Constitutional provision has been extended so that if the prosecution offers a deal to a suspected criminal by which he will not be prosecuted if he will testify against someone else, even if his testimony reveals his own criminal guilt, he is entitled to rely on that deal.

Grants of immunity have a long history, extending far back into the history of the common law. Where several people have been suspected of complicity in crime, it has long been the practice of the authorities to offer an immunity to one or two of them in order to obtain their testimony to convict the rest. A witness who has done this is said to have "turned state's evidence" - i.e. given the state the benefit of his evidence against his erstwhile colleagues. The frequency with which this is done, especially in serious crimes, leads one to doubt whether there is much honor among thieves. The incentive to a suspect to accept immunity is strong, because he will get off scot-free where his partners in crime may well draw heavy sentences. Of course that incentive is counter-balanced if the suspect believes that he will suffer reprisal from his partners or their friends as a result of testifying for the prosecution, a possibility that was discussed on page 52 in relation to the findings of the President's Commission on

Law Enforcement.

A suspect who does fear retribution from his criminal acquaintances will be put in a quandry if he is summoned to testify before a Grand Jury and offered immunity by the prosecutor, because there are decisions holding that a witness must answer questions put by a Grand Jury once he has been given immunity. In Re Grand Jury Investigation of Sam Giancana v. United States 352 F . 2d 921 (7th Cir . 1965), cert . denied 382 U .S . 959 indicated this to be so even if the questions asked by the Grand Jury are irrelevant. This leaves a witness before a Grand Jury with two alternatives, neither of which may appear very pleasant: (1) he may answer the questions put, with the result that the criminality of his colleagues is exposed, or (2) he may refuse to answer questions at all, and suffer conviction for contempt in refusing to answer. The latter alternative will shield any criminals of whom the witness has knowledge, but involves unpleasant sanctions and to that extent might be thought to impinge upon the privilege against self-incrimination. However, in Ullman v. United States 350 U .S . 422 (1956) the majority of the Supreme Court held, over a strong dissent by Justices Douglas and Black, that the Constitution did not grant a person a right to remain silent and that if immunity is offered to a witness he must tell what he knows.

It will have been noted from page 75 that the Fifth Amendment reads "No person . . .shall be compelled, in any criminal case, to be witness against himself . . . ." A literal interpretation of these words means that a person cannot be compelled to say anything self-incriminatory even in a trial of someone else, because the Amendment includes "any" criminal case. This has been the interpretation adopted by the Supreme Court, although there is some historical evidence to suggest that the framers of the Constitution intended only to prevent a defendant from being forced to confess in the presence of the court.

A prospective witness who may be vulnerable to prosecution in respect of something to which he may be asked to testify on the stand should, in his own interest, take legal advice in advance. In many cases immunity can be obtained without difficulty (at least in a criminal trial), but it must be sought beforehand. A witness who has not sought protection from subsequent prosecution cannot obtain it after the event. Of course he will have the option of claiming his privilege against self-incrimination if he has not obtained immunity, and upon hearing the claim the prosecution may respond by an offer of immunity while the case is proceeding, but it is probably to the benefit of all concerned that this should have been arranged in advance if possible. It will not be possible if the questions which invite the witness to incriminate himself are not anticipated, but this is relatively rare.

A grant of immunity does not include immunity from prosecution for perjury in respect of what is said. That is because immunity only relates to offenses committed prior to its grant, i.e. before the testimony is given. If that testimony is perjured the offense of perjury may be prosecuted; a grant of immunity is not a license to lie.

Chapter XIV

CROSS-EXAMINATION

Cross-examination has already been given considerable attention in this book, but it is so important that it justifies a chapter to itself. For one thing, it is the experience that witnesses fear most. For another, it is the most important characteristic of American courts, both civil and criminal. Lastly, it is an art which few members of the public have any real understanding of; it has been presented too often on the entertainment media as producing sensational results for an adept lawyer. In reality, cross-examination rarely provides the drama of surprise that is enacted almost nightly on the nation's television screens.

Cross-examination has been extravagantly praised as a great engine for the uncovering of deception, but its power may be doubted to be so strong, and is certainly rarely apparent in court. There are few lawyers who are truly skillful cross-examiners, and even fewer cases in which the exercise of skill will reveal anything important that was not known or at least suspected prior to trial. This is not to suggest that cross-examination is unimportant but rather to reduce its reputation to a sensible level. Demonstrably, cross-examination does not expose all that it might; because it is well recognized that perjury does take place which is never satisfactorily unmasked.

The technique of cross-examination is as often as not oblique - that is to say, that it adduces responses which are as significant for the inferences that can be drawn from them as for what is explicitly stated. This aspect of cross-examination is frequently the most annoying and frustrating for a witness, because he knows from the way that the questions are framed that they are designed to give the jury an impression which, from his point of view, is misleading.

Not all witnesses are used in this way. Many of them are not cross-examined at all; the evidence given on direct examination is accepted by the opposition. It follows that the more positive, damning testimony given on one side is likely to be cross-examined and challenged by the other side, because a "strong" witness on one side may in effect prove all, or most, of what the side calling him has to prove. To leave strong testimony unchallenged is to acknowledge its truth, from the jury's viewpoint.

A witness who gives positive testimony should not assume that the side which cross-examines him is being unfair in its methods of cross-examination. True, the questions he is asked will have been carefully chosen to reduce the impact or credibility of his evidence, but that is a basic right given by the rules to a legal contestant. It should be remembered that, in general, defendants are always at a tactical disadvantage because it is difficult to prove a negative. This applies to both civil and criminal trials.

Although cross-examination is a trial lawyer's most useful weapon, it does not follow from that that its efficacy to detect deliberate falsehood is great. Its utility lies far more in revealing witnesses' bias and "slanting" of the evidence since it must be generally assumed that witnesses naturally adopt a partisan attitude towards the trial for which they may be called, and lend their aid more willingly to one side rather than the other. This has nothing to do with the facts in their possession - facts are neutral - but rather reflects their sympathy with one party, or their emnity towards the other. If one side gets full and ready co-operation in preparing its case while the other does not, it stands to reason that the party receiving co-operation has a substantial advantage, which no legal rule can eliminate; it is a fact of life. Litigants associated with unpopular causes or who are themselves unpopular have found themselves the victims of this disadvantage many times.

A witness who finds his testimony solicited by both sides has the right to refuse to talk with either, or both of the parties, but he should not lightly agree to talk to one without talking to the other. To do so is to show clear favor to one side, and prejudge the merits of the litigation. It is one thing to hold strong views about what happened, but another to deliberately try to make the task of one side more difficult. A witness may fairly refuse to aid both sides, but not aid one while hindering another. In practice, many witnesses do the latter because they are told to by the attorney for one party, but that is not a command but only a request and the witness may do as he thinks fit. Neither side needs the permission of the other to interview prospective witnesses. It is an effective demonstration to the jury of the bias of a witness if a lawyer brings out on cross-examination that pre-trial interview was granted to the other side, but not to the side represented by the cross-examiner.

Problems of perspective affect every witness. The simple statement "He hit me" may be true, but may have a widely varying significance according to other data. Was the alleged assailant provoked? Was he hit first? Was he being threatened in some way? All these possibilities exist, but the person who suffered the blow is unlikely to acknowledge them or acknowledge their significance. To the extent that cross-examination aids in revealing a witness's 'blind-spots' of this type, it may uncover untruth, though not deception.

Some witnesses are cowed by the prospect of cross-examination, fearful that they will not make a good impression, and that they will be humiliated. Yet a witness does not need to make a good impression to be believed - what is important is that he does not make a bad one. Most witnesses are not skilled in the art of public relations or persuasion, and even if they were it is doubtful that they would make a universally favorable impression on their listeners. The cut and thrust of cross-examination does not lend itself to public relations consciousness on the part of the witness, for one of the purposes of cross-examination is to prevent a witness from giving carefully planned answers. The element of unpredictability in the questions is considered to be a means of revealing the witness as he "really" is - without a contrived and prepared set of answers to everything.

In practice, cross-examination does not even prevent experienced witnesses from giving pre-planned testimony. The thrust of most cross-examination can be anticipated and even if he is not intelligent a witness can get the drift of most cross-examinations from the first question or two.

There is no possibility of eliminating the "slanting" of evidence from our courts, by the use of cross-examination or otherwise, for under all the legality clothing of many lawsuits is the naked fact of a grudge, or vindictiveness, or simple dislike of someone who will suffer from the litigation. From the point of view of the litigant the unpleasantness of his opponent may be the true reason for his suit, and highly relevant; but it is not considered so by his counsel, or by the law itself. "Who knows what evil lurks in the hearts of men?" is not a question which the law tries to answer; spite, revenge, and other such emotions are ignored in court, unless they become overt.

The art of testimony cannot be reduced to a science; there are few universal rules and it is impossible to foresee every possibility on the witness-stand. Nevertheless, there are certain general principles which can aid a witness in all circumstances:

1. Keep your temper.

2. Answer a question in the shortest possible way,

3. Always be willing to admit ignorance of the subject-matter of a question, or that your memory has failed you, or that you are not sure,

4. Never show partiality, or vindictiveness, to either party to the litigation,

5. Never show reluctance to concede a point in the opposition's favor,

6. Use short, simple language so that your point is immediately comprehensible,

7. Ask for a question to be repeated or rephrased if you do not understand it.

A witness who acts according to these suggestions will not necessarily have an easy task, but he can rest assured that he will have performed his duty as a witness in a way that serves justice and does him credit as a citizen.

APPENDIX A

Subpoena to a Witness

Civil Court of	)	John Smith	PLAINTIFF
Hecate County,	)		
State of	)	v.	
New Connecticut	)		
	)	William Brown	DEFENDANT

To Thomas Jones, of 8 Railroad Avenue, Doddton, Hecate County, New Connecticut:

WHEREAS it has been made to appear that you are likely to be called to give material evidence in the above-entitled action for the plaintiff:

THIS COMMANDS YOU to attend the Civil Court of Hecate County on the first day of April, 1972, at ten o'clock in the forenoon at room 567 to hold yourself in readiness to give evidence in the above-entitled action.

DATED this twenty-fifth day of January, 1972, at Gadstone, Hecate County, New Connecticut.

Samuel Pettigrew
Clerk of the Court.

APPENDIX B

Warrant for Arrest of Witness

Civil Court of	)	John Smith	PLAINTIFF
Hecate County,	)		
State of	)	v.	
New Connecticut	)		
	)	William Brown	DEFENDANT

To The Sheriff of Hecate County:

WHEREAS a subpoena to appear for the purpose of testifying in the above-entitled action, dated the twenty-fifth day of January, 1972, at Gadstone, Hecate County, New Connecticut, was duly served on Thomas Jones, of 8 Railroad Avenue, Doddton, Hecate County, New Connecticut on the twenty-sixth day of January, 1972:

AND WHEREAS the said Thomas Jones failed to appear at the time, date and place indicated in said subpoena:

NOW THEREFORE, this commands you to bring the said Thomas Jones forthwith before the Civil Court of Hecate County.

DATED this twenty-fifth day of April, 1972, at Gadstone, Hecate County, New Connecticut

_____

Samuel Pettigrew
Clerk of the Court.

INDEX

LEGAL ALMANAC SERIES

Price Per Volume: $3.00, $3.50 for No. 9

Oceana Publications, Inc.

75 Main Street   **Dobbs Ferry, N.Y. 10522**